PROJECT
LEADERSHIP

The books in the Project Management Essential Library series provide project managers with new skills and innovative approaches to the fundamentals of effectively managing projects.

Additional titles in the series include:

Managing Project Integration, Denis F. Cioffi

The Triple Constraints in Project Management, Michael S. Dobson

Managing Projects for Value, John C. Goodpasture

Effective Work Breakdown Structures, Gregory T. Haugan

Project Planning and Scheduling, Gregory T. Haugan

Managing Project Quality, Timothy J. Kloppenborg and Joseph A. Petrick

Project Measurement, Steve Neuendorf

Six Sigma for Project Managers, Steve Neuendorf

Project Estimating and Cost Management, Parviz F. Rad

Project Risk Management: A Proactive Approach, Paul S. Royer

MANAGEMENTCONCEPTS

www.managementconcepts.com

PROJECT LEADERSHIP

Timothy J. Kloppenborg

Arthur Shriberg

Jayashree Venkatraman

MANAGEMENTCONCEPTS

Vienna, VA

ʍʍ
MANAGEMENTCONCEPTS

8230 Leesburg Pike, Suite 800
Vienna, VA 22182
(703) 790-9595
Fax: (703) 790-1371
www.managementconcepts.com

Printed in the United States of America

Library of Congress Cataloging-in-Publication Data

Kloppenborg, Timothy J., 1953–
    Project leadership / Timothy J. Kloppenborg, Arthur Shriberg, Jayashree Venkatraman.
        p. cm. — (The project management essential library)
    Includes bibliographical references and index.
    ISBN 1-56726-145-0 (pbk.)
        1. Project management. 2. Leadership. I. Shriberg, Arthur. II. Venkatraman, Jayashree, 1967– III. Title. IV. Series.

HD69.P75 K5983 2003
658.4'04—dc21

2002037863

About the Authors

Timothy J. Kloppenborg is a professor of Management at Williams College of Business, Xavier University, and President of Kloppenborg and Associates, a consulting and training company based in Cincinnati, Ohio, that specializes in project and quality management. He holds an MBA from Western Illinois University and a PhD in Operations Management from the University of Cincinnati. He is a Certified Project Management Professional (PMP®) and has been active in the Project Management Institute for more than 15 years. Dr. Kloppenborg has published in journals including *Project Management Journal*, *PM Network*, and *Quality Progress*. He also published another book in this series entitled *Managing Project Quality*. Dr. Kloppenborg is a retired United States Air Force Reserve officer. He has served in many practitioner, research, and consulting capacities on construction, information systems, and research and development projects.

Arthur Shriberg is a professor of Leadership at Xavier University. Dr. Shriberg has been vice president or dean at four universities. He has served as a consultant or training facilitator for 100 industrial, governmental, educational, and health care organizations. He is currently the chair of the Board of Commissioners for the Cincinnati Human Relations Commission and a senior consultant for Pope & Associates, an international diversity and management consulting firm. He is senior author of the textbook *Practicing Leadership: Principles and Application* as well as the author of numerous articles about leadership, management skills, and diversity. He holds degrees from the Wharton School of Business (BS), Xavier University (Executive Business), Boston University (MEd), and Teachers College, Columbia University (EdD).

Jayashree Venkatraman is an independent consultant providing business-to-business solutions and other software solutions to companies. She holds a BS in physics and an MS in computer applications from the University of

Madras, India, and an MBA from Xavier University. She also earned a certificate in Project Management from the University of Cincinnati. She has more than 12 years of experience in leading, designing, developing, implementing, and integrating software applications in a project environment for varied industries. She is a member of PMI®.

Table of Contents

Preface

People have performed projects all through history. Many of the great wonders of the ancient world required a generation or more to complete. While personal leadership often was essential to the completion of these huge projects, it was the exception rather than the rule.

In the early part of the twentieth century, management came to be studied as a formal discipline. Scientific management, management science, and many other developments led to the systemization of management concepts. This first generation approach was a great step forward, but it dealt primarily with managing ongoing operations.

Simultaneously during the second half of the twentieth century, leadership and project management evolved as separate disciplines. These second generation approaches dealt with inspiring workers and managing change. They represented another significant step forward. An explosion of ideas developed both in leadership and in project management—but largely independent of each other.

Now, early in the twenty-first century, we are reuniting these two disciplines into a third discipline: project leadership. Because of their temporary nature and unique output, projects are different from ongoing operations. For this reason, we synthesize a number of the leadership concepts and techniques that are especially relevant to projects and present them in a project lifecycle framework. This is truly a third generation approach to accomplishing project work.

The primary intended audience for this book is anyone who works in a project setting. We specifically address many of our suggestions to project sponsors, project managers, functional managers, project core team members, and project customers. Each has several important roles to play in project leadership.

A second intended audience for this book is any leader. Most people spend at least part of their time on projects. This book can be useful to help them adapt their leadership techniques and knowledge for use on projects.

This book starts by briefly outlining the roots of project leadership from management in the early twentieth century through project management and leadership during the late twentieth century. We specifically develop a project leadership model in which task, human resource, and commitment responsibilities are delineated.

The next four chapters of the book represent the stages in the four-stage project lifecycle: project initiating, project planning, project executing, and project closing. Each stage has a defined starting and ending point, with a sequence of activities that would normally be performed to lead a project through to its successful conclusion. The activities we describe are at a level of detail appropriate for a "middle of the road" project. A project that is simple, short, and familiar could be streamlined in the manner in which the activities are completed, but the spirit of the activities would still need to be accomplished. On a large, complex, or unfamiliar project, the activities would need to be performed in more detail. This "middle of the road" approach is designed to give project participants a good starting point from which to scale up or down.

Features included in this book to assist the reader include:

- An overall "science of project leadership" model to provide guidance on what project leadership responsibilities need to be accomplished at each stage in the four-stage project lifecycle
- A project case study that provides examples of what decisions need to be made at each point in the project's life
- Twenty-eight Project Leadership Lessons, which summarize each of the seven major project leadership challenges at each stage of a project
- Numerous figures and tables to help the reader visualize our ideas and tools.

The extent to which *Project Leadership* succeeds in presenting a useful model and adapted tools to our readers is our ultimate measure of success. Please let us know how this book has helped you in your work and where you think it could be improved. We welcome all your comments and examples.

Timothy J. Kloppenborg
Arthur Shriberg
Jayashree Venkatraman

Acknowledgments

We would like to thank Warren Opfer, who was an author of Chapter 5 and who developed the three Project Leadership Assessments. The authors would also like to thank Praxis Management International for their contribution in the development of the Project Leadership Assessments.

We thank our department (Management and Entrepreneurship Department, Williams College of Business at Xavier University) for the encouragement provided. We thank the following individuals for their assistance: Marjorie Shriberg, Shannon Borowski, Shirlee James, Donna Waymire, Rose Kutschbach, Joy Davis, and our many students who read drafts of the book. We also thank everyone at Management Concepts for their assistance in all aspects of the book, especially our editor Cathy Kreyche for her helpful comments and support.

We thank our parents; our wives, Elizabeth Kloppenborg and Marjorie Shriberg; and our children, Kathryn and Nicholas Kloppenborg, and David, Michael, Amy, Rebecca, and Steven Shriberg, for their patience, understanding, love, and support, which made this book possible.

Jayashree Venkatraman thanks her parents, Venkataraman Padmanabhan and Lakshmi Venkataraman; her sister, Parvatharavardhini Venkataraman; her brother, Ramakrishnan Venkataraman, and his wife Sabitha Ramakrishnan; her nephew Sanjay; Mr. Durairajan and family for their love and support; her friends who have supported her; and her co-authors for their encouragement and support.

Please let us know both how this book has helped you and how you think it can be improved.

Timothy J. Kloppenborg
kloppenb@xu.edu
(513) 745-4905 (home)
(513) 745-4383 (fax)

CHAPTER 1

The Origins of Project Leadership

I n this chapter we first discuss the basics of management and then review the two "children" of management that evolved in the latter part of the last century: leadership and project management. As we help the reader understand the basics of these three key disciplines, we will pave the way for discussion of a new approach that is evolving in the twenty-first century: project leadership. Figure 1-1 illustrates this evolution from management to project leadership.

MANAGEMENT

The practice of management, defined for many centuries as planning, organizing, directing, and controlling, has existed since early times. Building the Great Wall of China, running the Roman Empire, and preparing armies for battle all required management skills; until the late nineteenth century, however, management was usually viewed as an art that was passed on from generation to generation by oral tradition. In the last hundred years, the sci-

---

FIGURE 1-1   The Evolution of Project Management

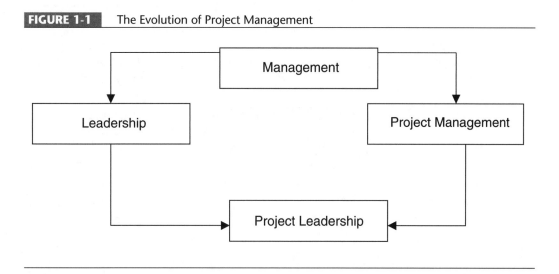

ence of management has developed. While management was once defined as "the ability work through others," today most definitions are similar to the one offered by Courtland Bouee, in his book *Management*: "Management is the process of attaining organizational goals by effectively and efficiently planning, organizing, leading and controlling the organization's human, physical, financial and informational resources."[1] This definition is presented graphically in Figure 1-2.

These four management activities can be described as:

- **Planning.** The process of creating goals and developing ways to achieve them has undergone dramatic changes in recent years as organizations have begun to think of goals and plans at three levels. *Strategic planning* is set at organizational levels and is usually of long duration. *Tactical planning* is set by middle managers to support corporate goals, is related to individual departments, and is usually of middle duration, often less than year. *Operational planning* is set by first-line management, to be achieved in the short run by individuals or departments.

- **Organizing.** The traditional method of organizing is by function or division. In recent years the trend has been to organize work by teams and networks with the aim of minimizing levels of decision-making. Organizations are flatter, and line and staff rules are being integrated in new ways.

FIGURE 1-2   The Elements of Management

Source: Based on Courtland Bouee, *Management* (New York: McGraw Hill, 1993), p. 5.

- **Leading.** Today, the whole question of the leader's role in ethical decision-making and responding to a wide variety of stakeholders—not just more senior leaders—is a central question.
- **Controlling.** We have moved from a very centralized controlling system to a model whereby every associate is in the quality control business. Continuous improvement is key in all organizations.

All these functions are now being viewed in the context of the organizational mission and values. The development of a statement of purpose or "mission statement," once just assumed to be profit maximization, is now a central and continuous function of management.

Throughout the twentieth century, several schools of management thought developed. These approaches, all of which still play a role, include the classical approach, the human relations movement, management science, systems theory, total quality management, and learning organizations.

The classic approach to management, also called "scientific management," focuses on the processes that workers use and attempts to find the best way to perform a task. We entered the industrial era seeking better (defined as more efficient) ways of doing things. Time and motion studies were the norm. Another aspect of this classical period in management was the evolution of classical organization theory—a school of thought that argued that work should be divided into logical functional areas, with each person having one boss. This led to the concept of bureaucracy, which was viewed as a means of ensuring productivity. The key aspects of bureaucracy (which over the years has taken on a negative connotation) are specialization of labor, formal procedures and rules, impersonal systems, clear hierarchy, and career advancement based on the quantity of productivity.

Many of these principles do not regard employees as human beings making specific contributions and having individual needs and concerns. As the century progressed, the human relations movement began. This movement stated that the path to success was through satisfying workers' basic needs, which would make the workers more productive. Behavioral scientists from a variety of disciplines helped companies understand that workers did indeed have different needs and, as these needs were satisfied, the workers became more productive. Maslow's hierarchy of needs, shown in Figure 1-3, still guides many decision-makers.

As we made progress in the mathematical sciences, the impact of the management science perspective grew. We learned that mathematical models and other statistical techniques could assist managers in making key decisions.

FIGURE 1-3   Maslow's Hierarchy of Needs

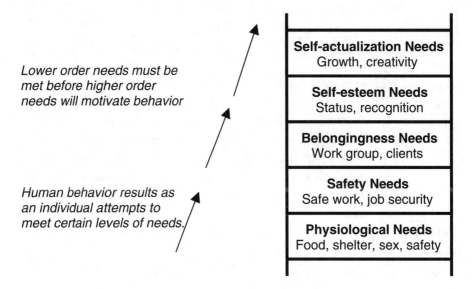

Source: Based on Arthur Shriberg, David Shriberg, and Carol Lloyd, *Practicing Leadership*, 2nd ed. (New York: Wiley & Sons, Inc., 2002, p. 23.

During World War II, several new approaches to management developed that are still called "contemporary management." The development of systems theory taught us that organizations are a set of interrelated parts that should function in a coordinated way to achieve a common goal. This led to a response that not all variables can be controlled and the development of a "contingency view," which states that managers often have to say "it depends" and make different decisions depending upon the particular situation.

The total quality movement began in the 1950s in Japan and did not truly come into vogue in the United States until the 1980s. The best known spokesperson for this movement, W. Edward Deming, developed a list of 14 points that must all be followed to ensure that total quality exists in an organization. Operationally, many managers have distilled the intent of Deming's list to: thoroughly understand all your customers, empower your employees, make decisions based on facts, and continually improve all your work processes.

Today, the concept of learning organizations has taken center stage. This concept implies that organizations are living entities that can learn, grow, and adapt to the environment. The more quickly organizations can change, the more likely it is that they will gain an advantage over their competitors.

Management has changed in many ways in the last hundred years, but all these theories are still practiced in many settings. It was in the last half of the twentieth century that leadership and project management began to evolve from management into separate disciplines.

LEADERSHIP

While there is substantial agreement on the elements and definition of management, there is little agreement on the definition of leadership, its functions, or even whether or not it is a discipline (although increasingly scholars agree that it is). Our favorite definition of leadership is: "an influence relationship among leaders and their collaborators, who intend real change that reflects their shared purpose."[2]

In his book *On Leadership*, John Gardner states that the functions of leadership are:

1. Envisioning goals
2. Affirming and regenerating important group values
3. Motivating others toward collective goals
4. Managing the process through which these collective goals can be achieved
5. Achieving unity of effort through pluralism and diversity
6. Creating an atmosphere of mutual trust
7. Explaining and teaching
8. Serving as a symbol of the group's identity
9. Representing the group's interest to outside parties
10. Renewing and adapting the organization to a changing world.[3]

We have identified ten different approaches to the study of leadership, as shown in Figure 1-4. Each is part of most leadership theories and each needs to be practiced in new ways in this century.

Trait Theory

It has long been accepted that, by studying the traits of others, we can learn how they function. After World War II, when the field of leadership began to emerge as a separate discipline, people often believed that the way to be an effective leader was to study others they perceived as effective. Biographies of leaders are plentiful. Studies of their various traits abound. Again, we

FIGURE 1-4 21st Century Approaches to the Study of Leadership

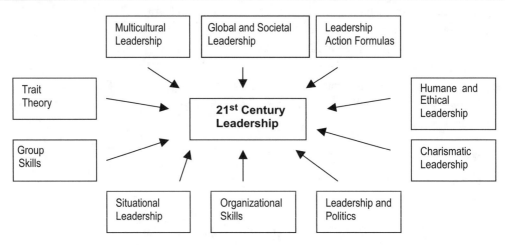

turn to Gardner, who teaches us that leaders most often have the following attributes:

1. Physical vitality and stamina
2. Intelligence and action-oriented judgment
3. Eagerness to accept responsibility
4. Task competence
5. Understanding of followers and their needs
6. Skills in dealing with people
7. Need for achievement
8. Capacity to motivate people
9. Courage and resolution
10. Trustworthiness
11. Decisiveness
12. Self-confidence
13. Assertiveness
14. Adaptability.[4]

While others may choose different traits, these types of traits have always been valued. Daniel Goldman, in his highly acclaimed work, *The Handbook of Emotional Intelligence*, teaches us that self-awareness, self-regulation, motivation, empathy, and social skills are the keys to being a great leader.[5]

Group Skills

Groups need information givers, gatekeepers, consensus builders, and many other roles to be filled. Courses in group dynamics are taught in an effort to develop these skills.

Today the emphasis is on how to turn a group into a team and on ensuring that the team empowers all its members to be effective and productive in implementing shared goals. Organizational workers (often called associates or partners) are increasingly being encouraged to build effective teams and to provide input into all aspects of the teams' goals. While at one time most people were evaluated solely on their individual productivity, the concept of mutual dependence is growing; each year more of us are evaluated at last in part based on the productivity of our "team."

The modern leader understands that effective teams have interdependent members. The productivity and efficiency of an entire unit is determined by the coordinated, interactive efforts of all its members.

Advantages of effective teams include:
- Members are more efficient working together than alone.
- Teams create their own magnetism.
- Leadership rotation allows those with expertise to lead.
- Team members care for and nurture one another.
- Each member gives and receives mutual encouragement.
- Members share a high level of trust.

If a team is to be successful, its leader needs to understand how teams develop and what is expected at each stage of team development.

Situational Leadership

The situational leadership theory tells us that the directing, coaching, supporting, and delegating styles of leadership are all needed at different times. The original view stated that the needs of the followers dictate the necessary leadership style, as shown in Figure 1-5.

Organizational Skills

Traditionally leaders have been expected to know how to organize things in an efficient manner. They make sure that people have one boss, clear directions, etc. They develop organizational charts that are clean and easy to understand, choosing either a functional or a divisional structure with clearly defined lines of authority. Strategic, functional, and operational plans and goals are carefully developed. Leaders know the "rules" of creating an orga-

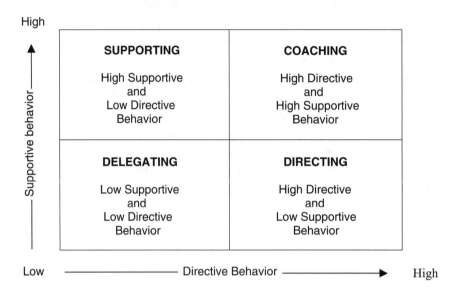

FIGURE 1-5 Situational Leadership

Adapted from Paul Hersey and Kenneth Blanchard, *Management of Organizational Behavior*, 4th ed. (Englewood Cliffs, NJ: Prentice Hall Inc.), 1982, p. 152.

nization that works and they do it well. They understand how to function within their role in the organization, and they slowly and appropriately move up in the organizational hierarchy.

All these guidelines may still apply, but in this century leaders live in "permanent white water." Organizations are matrixed, team-based, networked, or organized in some unique way. Traditional pyramids are being inverted. Change may be the only constant. While it is useful to understand traditional organizational skills, it is also necessary to realize that flexibility and speed are often the new rules. The ways to lead an organization effectively are as varied as the number of people with positional power in that organization.

Leadership and Politics

Traditionally leadership was taught as a subset of the field of politics. The key concept was power and the challenge to leaders was to use power wisely.

Understanding how to use legitimate power (the power that comes with a position or title), the power to reward, and the power to punish was the basis of leadership.

Today we talk about referent power—how people view or respect other people. This power cannot be delegated or assigned, but must be earned. We also value expert power, which is found throughout any organization and is the ability to understand or do something well. Instead of "power over," we discuss empowerment or "power with." Sam Walton built Wal-Mart by empowering his associates to run a "store within a store."

Power is also often examined in terms of minority groups who lack the power of the majority. Throughout the second part of the twentieth century we discussed "black power," "women power," "gay power," and other groups who are "disempowered" and seeking a change. Successful leaders understand that power needs to be shared and that empowered people are productive people.

Charismatic Leadership

In the mid-twentieth century we had many charismatic leaders, such as John F. Kennedy, Franklin Roosevelt, Winston Churchill, Lee Iacocca, Billy Graham, and Jackie Robinson. Jay Conger defines a charismatic leader as "someone who possesses an ability to introduce quantum changes in an organization."[6] He indicates that these people take the organization through four steps:

1. Sensing opportunities and finding vision
2. Articulating the vision
3. Building trust in the vision
4. Achieving the vision.

So far in this century there appears to be a dearth of charismatic leaders. In the last five years we have asked more than one thousand students to name charismatic leaders; rarely is a current leader mentioned. However, in a recent national study, one third of the people who indicated that they "enjoy" their work stated that their boss or company leaders were charismatic. Clearly, leaders can be successful without charisma, but it is also true that charisma is a helpful trait if used properly. There is a dark side of charisma, however, as Hitler, bin Laden, and others have demonstrated. In the twentieth century perhaps a fifth element should be added to Conger's definition: choosing a vision that advances humankind in a positive direction.

Humane and Ethical Leadership

In the 1980s a trend developed that considered the only true leaders to be those who were ethical and humane. The prevailing view was that a leader needs to be ethically grounded and a person of integrity.

The current crisis in confidence in our institutions also requires leaders to hold ethical standards that create win/win situations for everyone. The challenge is to solve problems in the long run. Respecting the individual becomes a key measure of a leader.

Today we respect work/life balance and we expect leaders to respect the individual needs of all associates. Leaders are expected to promote healthy behavior of all sorts in the organization. The ethical leader treats all people fairly but not the same. Leaders at all levels are expected to be ethical and humane and are often held to higher standards than they were in the past.

Humane leaders are also humane followers; they understand that to lead well, one must also follow well.

Leadership Action Formulas

Bookstores have been filled with "how to lead" books for close to a century. While these books once were formulaic and rule-driven, they now reflect the complexity of leading in a modern world. Many famous athletes, corporate leaders, and government officials have written books about leadership, from Maxwell's 21 irrefutable laws of leadership[7] to Larry Holman's 11 lessons in self-leadership.[8]

In recent years, however, the books have taken a different twist. Perhaps Covey's *7 Habits of Highly Successful People* began this change. Covey's best-seller and his many books since stress internal change: "the person becomes the leader of the future by an inside out transformation." Covey's seventh habit—sharpening the saw—is an example of current leadership advice that asks readers to find balance in all aspects of life.[9]

One of the newer approaches to leadership formulas is a shift to using metaphors to "teach" leadership. Blanchard and several colleagues have written about "raving fans," "gung-ho," and "whale done," using these metaphoric experiences to inform readers about some aspects of leadership.[10]

Global and Societal Leadership

Most of the leadership literature in the last century discusses leadership primarily within the context of U.S. culture and Christian values. For the vast majority of leaders, however, this is no longer the reality. Less than 5 percent of the world lives in the United States. More people speak three languages than speak English. Christianity is practiced by less than 30 percent of the world. Most companies have customers, suppliers, or workers from other countries and other cultures. Leadership is a cultural phenomenon and is practiced in very different ways in different cultures. Wise leaders understand that they must listen to, respond to, and learn from stakeholders with very different concepts of leadership based upon their cultural heritage and experience.

Multicultural Leadership

The concept of the "melting pot" dominated much of the twentieth century: Leaders were taught to find commonalities and "blend" differences. If people were different because they spoke a different language or had a different outlook or experiences in life, these "handicaps" were to be overcome.

We now understand that we live in a "salad" or "fruit bowl," where the texture, depth, and beauty of our society come from the differences people bring to an organization. We leverage these differences to make better and more creative decisions.

There are many subcultures in our society and the buying power of many groups is skyrocketing. We need "soccer moms" to help us understand and meet the needs of other "soccer moms" just as we need Hispanic or Islamic people to help us understand how the fastest growing ethnic and religious groups in the United States think and experience life. This understanding requires flexibility, a constant willingness to grow and change, and openness to continually evolving definitions of leadership.

PROJECT MANAGEMENT

Just as events throughout history have required management and leadership, many have required what has become known as project management. A project is a temporary undertaking to produce a unique output subject to limitations such as time, people, and other resources. Projects have occurred all through recorded history. Construction projects have included the pyramids of Egypt, the great cathedrals of Europe, and the temple at Machupicchu. Research and development projects included the creation of metals during the Bronze Age and the development of war implements during many ages. Projects were conducted to wage war and to build civilizations. These examples all qualify as projects since they were temporary endeavors that created unique outputs subject to limitations. It is highly unlikely that the people performing these projects shared lessons about what worked since they were generally separated by distance, time, and war. Because there was no open sharing, however, project management did not exist as a formal discipline.

The resulting lack of professionalism in early project management can be highlighted by asking questions about the success of these projects: Was the output produced efficiently and effectively? Were any of the limitations exceeded? Were the "customers" satisfied? What did the stakeholders think of the project? While we may never know the answers to these questions, we can guess on some of them. Some of these projects required the efforts of thousands of people (often slaves). Some required large amounts of time—more than a century in some cases. Many of the project participants (especially slaves) were probably far from satisfied with the work demands placed on them. The outputs of some of the projects were probably successful, but the outputs of others certainly were not.

Management principles that had developed previously applied generally to ongoing operations. Projects are different in that, once their objective is achieved, they are (or should be) disbanded. The temporary nature of projects created different kinds of management challenges that were increasingly not being met using traditional management principles alone.

By the middle of the twentieth century, many began to believe that there must be a better way to achieve the desired results of projects. With the advent of World War II, the demands of war required that projects be completed very rapidly. Shortages of people and materials required the careful use of resources. In 1957, the Soviet Union successfully launched a satellite, Sputnik. This event signaled the need for a wide range of new developments that are collectively known as the Space Race. The desire for a successful moon landing translated into a very large project with specific goal and time limitations. The need for project management became crystal clear.

In 1969 the Project Management Institute (PMI®) was organized to allow project managers to share experiences. The premise behind PMI® is that projects share certain similarities regardless of size, complexity, or industry, and that the skills needed to manage projects are fundamentally different from those needed to manage ongoing work processes.

In the 1970s, much effort was spent developing cost and schedule controls and automated project management software. In 1987 PMI® published the first edition of *A Guide to the Project Management Body of Knowledge* (*PMBOK®*). The *PMBOK®* continued to develop and broaden with increased emphasis on topics such as risk, quality, human resources, and communications. The most recent addition to the *PMBOK®* is project integration—tying together all the project areas into a unified, workable plan.

In the 1990s, project management increased its focus on communications, team building, leadership development, and motivation. The specific areas in which the project management discipline increased its focus during the 1990s include:

- Stakeholder identification and management
- Project team member competency and commitment
- Interpersonal/behavioral aspects
- Communications and communications planning
- Performance measurement to specifications/objectives
- Integration of core and ad hoc team personnel
- Project management as a career path.

Definition of Project Management

So what is this thing called project management? Understanding it requires the definition of a project. According to PMI®, "A project is a temporary endeavor undertaken to create a unique product or service."[11] This brief definition suggests several notions. First, because the output is a unique product or service, project personnel must develop a thorough understanding of what that output is, along with the limitations and risks that will be encountered in trying to achieve it. Second, because a project is temporary it must be handled differently from an ongoing operation. In particular, the project lifecycle must be understood. Finally, both the temporary nature and the unique output of a project create the need for alternative forms of organization and for unique project skills and tools.

"Project management is the application of skills, tools, and techniques to project activities to meet project requirements."[12] This requires project managers to understand the project objectives, limitations, lifecycle, and roles of the participants. It also suggests that project managers should possess a variety of essential skills.

Every project has an objective, that is, a reason for performing the project. This objective can be implementing a new computer system, constructing a building, merging two companies, or developing a new product. Each objective has two considerations: scope (the features that are included) and quality (how the output performs).

Every project also has one or more limitations on how well and how quickly the objectives can be achieved. These limitations frequently include budget, resources, time, and technology. The limitations create risks that the objectives may not be met; these risks need to be identified.

Project Lifecycle

Unlike ongoing operations that continue indefinitely, projects are temporary and have lifecycles. A project lifecycle can be used to guide a project team through all the necessary work. Some industries have their own, highly detailed project lifecycle models. However, a simple four-stage model (shown in Figure 1-6) can be used to explain the concept.

The first stage, *initiating*, starts with identifying a potential project. Initiating activities include establishing the need for the project, understanding the project scope, approximating the time and cost required, and securing approval to plan the project in detail.

Once approval is granted, the project enters the *planning* stage. Many additional details are planned, some team members are added, and approval to perform the project work is granted.

The third stage, *executing*, is when most of the project work is accomplished. The project team is at its maximum size. Activities are directed, monitored, and controlled. This stage ends when the project customer accepts the project output.

The final stage—*closing*—occurs when workers and other resources are reassigned; the project is evaluated and administratively closed.

Several distinct roles are required for projects. A project manager is responsible for ensuring that the objectives are accomplished. This requires facilitating the project team, dealing with problems, making decisions (often

FIGURE 1-6	Project Lifecycle Model

Stage	Initiating	Planning	Executing	Closing
Level of Effort				
Stage-ending deliverable	Approval to plan project	Approval to execute project	Project output accepted	Administrative closure

concerning tradeoffs between the project objectives and limitations), and communicating with all other parties. A sponsor (usually an executive) guides the project manager and helps behind the scenes with overcoming obstacles. The project team determines the details of how the work must proceed, performs the work, and reports progress. Stakeholders are those who have an interest in the project. The primary stakeholder is the customer of the output, but many other parties also have interests in a project. For example, neighbors at a construction site may have concerns about noise, dust, and traffic.

A project manager must possess a variety of skills to achieve the project objectives. According to Kloppenborg and Mantel (2001), these skills can be grouped generally into six categories: planning, budgeting, scheduling, resourcing, monitoring, and controlling.[13] While managers of ongoing operations also need to perform tasks related to each of these six categories, the methods by which these must be performed on projects are different because of the temporary nature and the unique output that define projects. Many project-specific, specialized skills in these areas have been developed over time.

PROJECT LEADERSHIP

Pulling together the science of project management with effective leadership judgment is the essence of project leadership. The dizzying array of suggestions for leadership combined with the time-sensitive project completion challenges create a need for a new model. The model we have developed offers guidance on how and when to apply leadership principles to the various stages of a project. We define project leadership as the systematic application of leadership understanding and skills at each stage of a project lifecycle.

Project Lifecycle

All projects have a lifecycle. That is, there are certain predictable events that will take place in the life of every project. The wise project leader will understand this lifecycle and plan for it. The alternative is to be surprised (often unpleasantly and quite frequently) when leading a project. Understanding the project lifecycle is part of the science of project leadership in that it can be studied, there is a definite process that can be followed, and project leaders can learn what they need to do at each stage.

We use a very simple, generic project lifecycle model. We understand that many industries have unique demands that may suggest the use of more involved lifecycle models. However, the basic stages we identify and the project leadership tasks that must be accomplished during each stage will apply to most projects in most industries. Projects in certain industries may have additional unique project leadership responsibilities. Even on very small, simple projects, however, the intent of the responsibilities identified needs to be understood and accomplished. By understanding the most typical project leadership responsibilities, a skilled project leader can scale up or down the complexity depending on the project he or she is leading.

The simple lifecycle model we are using has four stages: initiating, planning, executing, and closing. Each stage contains one or more stage-ending deliverables that must be approved or accepted before proceeding to the next stage (as shown in Figure 1-6).

Figure 1-7 shows the level of effort that is needed by each type of leader at each stage of the project lifecycle. The horizontal axis shows how the stages follow each other over time. The length of the stages may vary widely depending on the project. The vertical axis shows the amount of effort (measured either in person hours of work or in dollars expended per time period). Note

FIGURE 1-7 Project Leaders' Level of Effort over the Project Lifecycle

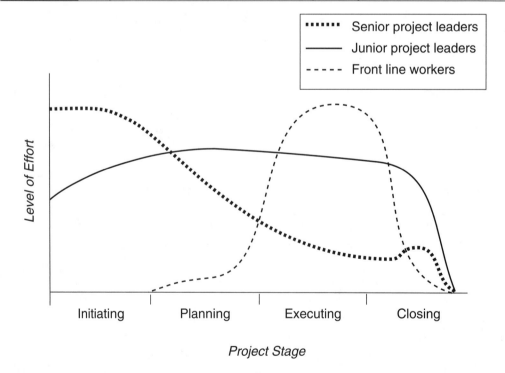

that the effort expended by senior project leaders is highest during project initiation, diminishes during planning and execution, and finally rises a bit during project closing. Junior leaders may be selected during the initiation stage or even the planning stage and may start their involvement with heavy effort right away. Junior leaders' effort, while highest during planning and execution, remains high throughout the project. Front-line workers' effort starts quite low, builds during planning, is by far highest during implementation, and decreases sharply during closure.

When considering the enthusiasm and team building necessary for a project team, one needs to remember that project participants can have very different patterns of participation. Senior leaders often go through the various team-building emotions a stage before junior leaders, who in turn go through the team-building emotions a stage before the front-line workers. A wise project leader will understand situational leadership and team development and then apply those lessons with great care depending on what individuals need.

Types of Project Leadership Decisions

The stage-specific project leadership tasks are shown in Table 1-1. Note that the three types of issues project leaders face relate to a variety of task, personnel, and commitment situations. All leaders must face many of these same issues. The issues are more complex in projects than in ongoing operations because projects have exceptional demands, particularly as a result of their temporary nature and unique outputs. Understanding the decisions that project leaders must make is also part of the science of project leadership because it is prescriptive—that is, these decisions must be made. The decisions identified in Table 1-1 will form the basis of the following chapters.

Project leaders have three types of task responsibilities. First, leaders must determine priorities and continue to insist that those priorities are adhered to. Second, project leaders continually need to be aware of project details and make decisions related to changing conditions. Finally, project leaders need to see and communicate how this project integrates into the grander scheme of things—both within the parent organization and in the customer's organization.

Personnel responsibilities are both procedural and behavioral. Procedural (human resource) issues include selecting and hiring project participants, supervising their work, and ensuring that they have future employment after the project is complete. Behavioral (human relations) responsibilities include helping the project core team develop operating and communication meth-

TABLE 1-1 Stage-Specific Project Leadership Tasks

Category of Project Leadership Task	Project Leadership Stage			
	Initiating	**Planning**	**Executing**	**Closing**
Project Priorities	Align project with parent organization	Understand and respond to the customer	Authorize work	Audit project
Project Details	Perform risk analysis	Oversee detailed plan development	Monitor progress and control changes	Terminate project
Project Integration	Justify and select project	Integrate project plans	Coordinate work across multiple projects	Capture and share lessons learned
Human Resources	Select key project participants	Select remainder of project participants	Supervise work performance	Reassign workers
Human Relations	Determine team operating methods	Develop communications plan	Lead teams	Reward and recognize participants
Project Promotion	Develop top management support	Motivate all participants	Maintain morale	Celebrate project completion
Project Commitment	Commit to project	Secure key stakeholder approval	Secure customer acceptance	Oversee administrative closure

ods, leading teams, and ensuring that worthy participants are recognized for their efforts.

Successful projects require many different stakeholders to make and keep commitments. A project leader has the responsibility of advocating the project in such a way that each concerned individual will want to make and keep the necessary project commitments. If this "unofficial advocacy" is done well, the official signing of documents should be easy.

THE BUSINESS TO BUSINESS (B2B) PROJECT CASE STUDY

Since the art of project leadership requires that project leaders develop judgment in making decisions, we use a fictitious case study to serve as an example of how these decisions are made. Experience on one project will not give a new project leader all the judgment that is needed, but it is a start. We use the case study to demonstrate the thought process a project leader must use.

California Semiconductor Manufacturers (CSM), based in the suburbs of Sacramento, California, is the largest dedicated independent semiconductor company in the United States. Companies around the world have trusted CSM as an integrated circuit (IC) manufacturing services company since it was formed in 1992. CSM provides a range of manufacturing services, including design services, wafer probing, assembly, and testing. Market pressures for shorter concept-to-product lifecycle, higher product quality, and ever-increasing technology needs are causing more and more customers to turn to CSM as their partner.

CSM's vision is to be the most reputable, service-oriented, and profitable "fab" (i.e., fabricator of silicon wafers). CSM strives to be the virtual fab to its customers by providing the services and technologies the customers would demand if they owned and operated their own manufacturing facilities. CSM's intent is to make the foundry service as transparent as possible by providing a seamless relationship with its customers and thus giving them the advantages of having their own fabrication facilities without the associated costs.

CSM provides manufacturing services to semiconductor companies, integrated device manufacturers, and systems equipment manufacturing companies that need fabrication services. By providing access to those companies, it allows small and emerging firms to bring new IC designs to the market. Integrated device manufacturers turn to foundries like CSM to manufacture some of their device portfolios. Systems equipment manufacturing companies outsource IC manufacturing to fabricators like CSM so that they can concentrate on their core systems and software competency.

CSM is the industry's largest manufacturer of wafers, producing about 8 percent of all wafers. CSM strives to be the capacity leader and has adopted aggressive capacity expansion plans and consistent volume production levels. As capacity and market leader, CSM is well positioned in the marketplace.

CSM offers a wide range of next-generation IC process technologies. These technologies include the advanced CMOS logic process, advanced SRAM/embedded SRAM process, advanced flash/embedded flash memory process, mixed signal process, and advanced embedded DRAM process.

Business Model

CSM practices a customer-first business model that combines CSM's customer-oriented business strategy with its pioneering dedicated IC experience, management's commitment to customer satisfaction, and a systematic approach to responding immediately to customers' needs. CSM works to help make its customers competitive in the marketplace, achieving success through its customers' success.

Business Philosophy

CSM's business philosophy is based on:

- Integrity
- Building quality into all aspects of business
- Maintaining consistent focus on its core business
- Treating customers as partners
- Fostering innovation
- Fostering a dynamic and fun work environment
- Caring for employees and shareholders and being a good corporate citizen.

Management Team

CSM's executive team consists of Mark Taylor, CEO and founder; Gary Short, CIO; Peter Lee, Vice President of Engineering; Carl Mathew, CFO; Susan Park, Vice President of marketing; and Bob McCally, Vice President of sales and operations. Mark Taylor formed the company in 1992 and under his leadership the company has grown from 10 employees in 1992 to 8,000 employees currently. He believes in quality management and emphasizes quality throughout the organization.

Gary Short joined the company in 1997 and is responsible for all technological decisions. He believes that technology applied well can improve supply chain time and can provide better return on investment for the company. He is very actively involved as a volunteer in the community.

Peter Lee joined the company in 1996 and has led the engineering team to success, helping the company increase its product lines and its design services. Originally from Taiwan, he earned his PhD in Engineering at Caltech.

Susan Park joined the company in 1996. She leads the marketing organization.

Bob McCally joined the company in 1995 and has increased sales revenue by 70 percent since then. Achievement-oriented, Bob emphasizes setting challenging goals and high expectations to improve performance. He believes that project leaders have many important decisions to make and need help in developing their judgment.

Operational Highlights of CSM

CSM has a single-minded focus on the silicon wafer industry. The company provides high quality IC manufacturing services to the semiconductor industry. Building on its core competencies of manufacturing and excellent customer support, CSM offers wafer manufacturing, wafer probing, IC assembly and testing, and mask production. CSM has responded to customer needs for increased efficiency in the supply chain by providing an online system for customers who want greater control over their design cycle and manufacturing process.

With 8,000 employees, CSM places priority on developing employees and gaining their commitment. CSM focuses on employee satisfaction and fostering a dynamic and fun work environment. The company subscribes to a philosophy of lifelong learning and partnering with local universities for employee development. Through the company's performance management and development process, CSM has a defined method for maximizing every employee's potential.

> Now that we have introduced the key project leadership practices, the project lifecycle, and the fictitious B2B project case, we will spend the next four chapters demonstrating the kinds of decisions project leaders need to make. Our method will be to have the CSM project leaders make decisions at each project stage. Then we will comment on these decisions. We will summarize our comments regarding each decision with a project leadership lesson. Our goal is to offer readers useful suggestions in tackling their own projects.

NOTES

1. Courtland Bouee, *Management* (New York: McGraw Hill, 1993), p. 95.
2. Arthur Shriberg, David Shriberg, and Carol Lloyd, *Practicing Leadership: Principles and Applications*, 2nd ed. (New York: Wiley & Sons, Inc., 2002).
3. John William Gardner, *On Leadership* (New York: Free Press, 1990).
4. Ibid.
5. Daniel Goldman, *The Handbook of Emotional Intelligence: Theory, Development, Assessment, and Application at Home, School and in Work Place* (San Francisco, CA: Jossey-Bass, 2000).
6. Jay Alden Conger, *Charismatic Leadership in Organizations* (Thousand Oaks, CA: Sage Publications, 1998).
7. John Maxwell, *The 21 Irrefutable Laws of Leadership* (Nashville, TN: Thomas Nelson Publishers, 1998).
8. Larry Holman, *Eleven Lessons in Self-Leadership: Insights for Personal and Professional Success* (Lexington, KY: A Lessons in Leadership Book, 1995).
9. Stephen Covey, *The 7 Habits of Highly Successful People* (New York: Simon & Schuster, 1990).
10. Ken Blanchard, *Whale Done!* (New York: Free Press, 2002); Ken Blanchard and Sheldon Bowles, *Gung Ho: Turn on the People in Any Organization* (New York: William Morrow and Company, Inc., 1988); Ken Blanchard and Sheldon Bowles, *Raving Fans: A Revolutionary Approach to Customer Service* (New York: Free Press, 1993).
11. Project Management Institute, *A Guide to the Project Management Body of Knowledge (PMBOK® Guide)*, 2000 edition (Newtown Square, PA: Project Management Institute, 2000), p. 4.
12. Ibid., p. 6.
13. Timothy J. Kloppenborg and Samuel J. Mantel, Jr. "Project Management," *The Concise International Encyclopedia of Business and Management*, 2nd ed. (London: Thompson Press, 2001), p. 5438.

CHAPTER 2

Project Initiating

P roject leaders have responsibilities related to setting and enforcing priorities, ensuring that project details are planned and executed, and ensuring integration both within and outside the project. They are also responsible for the formal human resources and personal human relations aspects of acquiring, overseeing, and rewarding project personnel. Project leaders also need to promote the project in order to secure and maintain the commitments of key project stakeholders at each stage in the project lifecycle. These responsibilities are summarized in Table 2-1, with the initiating stage highlighted.

Chapters 2–5 cover the four project lifecycle stages. Each will be divided into the seven major categories of project leader responsibilities. Each section

TABLE 2-1 Project Leader Responsibilities: Initiating

Category of Project Leadership Task	Project Leadership Stage			
	Initiating	**Planning**	**Executing**	**Closing**
Project Priorities	Align project with parent organization	Understand and respond to the customer	Authorize work	Audit project
Project Details	Perform risk analysis	Oversee detailed plan development	Monitor progress and control changes	Terminate project
Project Integration	Justify and select project	Integrate project plans	Coordinate work across multiple projects	Capture and share lessons learned
Human Resources	Select key project participants	Select remainder of project participants	Supervise work performance	Reassign workers
Human Relations	Determine team operating methods	Develop communications plan	Lead teams	Reward and recognize participants
Project Promotion	Develop top management support	Motivate all participants	Maintain morale	Celebrate project completion
Project Commitment	Commit to project	Secure key stakeholder approval	Secure customer acceptance	Oversee administrative closure

will start by demonstrating project leaders' challenges using the fictitious example of the company introduced in the case study, California Semiconductor Manufacturers (CSM). The project leadership considerations will be presented to help project leaders use the CSM project to assist them in resolving real-life issues on their own projects.

Each section will be summarized with a project leadership lesson displayed inside a box. The lesson will be titled with the project stage column and the category of leadership task row that correspond to the specific cell shown in Table 2-1. For example, the first lesson applies to aligning the project with the parent organization. This deals with the initiating stage and the project priorities row, so it is labeled Initiating—Project Priorities.

Project leaders usually do not finish one responsibility before starting another; there is often considerable overlap and interaction between and among various responsibilities. For simplicity we will present project leaders' responsibilities in as close to a logical order as possible. First we will concentrate on the task responsibilities: Leaders need to have an understanding of the project work before they know what type of personnel, how many, and when each will be needed. Each project stage will culminate in a commitment of some kind.

Our coverage of the first project stage, *initiating*, starts with the project priority task of aligning the project with the parent organization, the project detail task of performing a risk assessment, and the project integration task of justifying and selecting the project. Next is the human resources task of selecting key project participants and the human relations task of determining project team operating methods. Finally the project leaders must complete the project promotion task of securing top management support and the commitment task of securing the public and personal commitment of each key project participant, often in the form of a signed charter.

If a project leader successfully shepherds a project through these seven project initiation tasks, the project will be ready to proceed into the planning stage (covered in Chapter 3). If the project leaders cannot successfully complete all project initiation tasks, maybe it is a poorly conceived project that does not deserve to be planned and executed. One reason for the project initiation stage is to quickly (and inexpensively) weed out inferior projects, so the failure of some projects to proceed further should be expected.

ALIGN THE PROJECT WITH THE PARENT ORGANIZATION

Using our B2B case study as our working example, Terry (VP of worldwide sales and operations of Buslog Technologies) sent Bob (VP of sales and operations at CSM) an e-mail stating that they would like to implement an automated business-to-business processing system using CSM's ordering systems. Since Buslog is one of CSM's most important customers, this e-mail caught Bob's attention. Terry also mentioned that they would provide a software license for CSM to use and would be willing to work with CSM's technical and sales organization to implement this project. Terry invited Bob and his company's executive team to attend a presentation by Buslog Technologies to its primary vendors to ask for their participation in reducing supply chain inefficiencies. Gary (CIO) and Bob attended the presentation.

After the presentation, Bob and Gary agreed that they would like to participate in the Phase I implementation and that CSM should be committed to this project. Mark (CSM's CEO) scheduled an executive team meeting to discuss the project. Mark asked Gary and Bob to work together to come up with a short presentation of what the project could mean to CSM and why they should take it on. In their presentation Gary and Bob pointed out that this B2B project would be the beginning of a strategic *customer integration initiative*. This customer integration initiative would eventually include implementing an enterprise resource planning (ERP) system that could, in turn, yield many additional benefits to the company.

In summary, Bob and Gary proposed that, if the executive team selected this project, the project mission would be to develop automated B2B processing between the CSM and Buslog ordering systems.

Project Leadership Considerations

A project leader's first task is to ensure that a project to be undertaken aligns with the parent organization. This consists of several activities, the first of which is to assess the culture, teamwork, risk tolerance, communications, decision-making, and trust levels in the overall organization to determine how capable the overall organization is in supporting project leadership. It is important to understand strengths and weaknesses and to develop ways to improve upon past performance. Apendix A contains a project leadership assessment tool that is designed to assist in analyzing and evaluating project leadership at the organizational level.

Effective project leadership requires proper attitudes, skills, and competencies. It is a willingness to take personal risk—to show genuine concern for the company, client, project, and everyone involved. The good news is that most of the skills and competencies required to be a successful project leader can be learned and that coaching and mentoring are instrumental in a leader's development.

The individual, team, and organizational aspects of leadership are interdependent. Senior management support establishes a foundation for leadership success, but it is the application of leadership characteristics at the individual and team levels that makes it truly effective.

The assessment questionnaire provides a self-scored assessment of the state of project leadership at the organizational level. This is not designed to answer all the questions that need to be asked for effective project leadership, but rather to provide an indicator for further action.

Once it is determined that the organization is ready to support project leadership, the next step in alignment is to identify potential projects. Ideally, all leaders in an organization are continually searching for potential projects as part of their everyday work.

The third step is to assess each potential project. Some large organizations may have extensive assessment procedures, while some small organizations may have almost none. Regardless of the size of the organization or the complexity of the project, a few key questions should be asked to determine if a potential project might align well with the parent organization's priorities:

- What is the project's vision?
- What value does the potential project offer the organization?
- Can the project be understood and articulated at different levels (as part of the larger organization, as a system itself, and as a combination of its parts)?
- What level of human and other resources will the project potentially require?
- What is the project's priority in comparison with other projects?
- How is work within the project prioritized?
- How will the parent organization's culture help or hinder the work of this project and vice versa?

CSM's top officers acknowledged that several benefits could come from this project and that it was consistent with a company philosophy of partnering with customers. However, the leaders did not spend enough time assessing whether the company had and could use the human and other resources necessary to complete this project, nor did they assess the impact this project would have on CSM's overall mission, vision, and goals. Many projects when considered in isolation appear to be a good fit; however, wise leaders consider potential projects in comparison with each other when making alignment decisions.

The automated B2B processing project under consideration at CSM appears to be a good fit in that it has the enthusiastic support of one of the company's major customers and will have many other benefits to CSM. The executive team seems excited and willing to work hard to help the project succeed. Direct benefits to CSM include better shipment notice information and reduced product lead time, both of which will have a positive impact on customer service. Since the project appears to be a good fit, CSM's project leaders are now ready to proceed into their second responsibility, which is to perform a risk assessment.

Project Leadership Lesson: Initiating—Project Priorities
A Project Leader Needs to:
Accept the strengths and weaknesses of both the parent company's organization and this potential project
Have the courage to assess how well this project will actually help the parent company achieve its goals
Exercise the wisdom to accept or reject this project accordingly.

PERFORM RISK ANALYSIS

At CSM a special team of assessment experts independently performs risk analysis and makes project selection recommendations. This assessment team met with the executive team to identify project risks and their impact. The list of risks the team identified is shown in Table 2-2.

The steering committee argued that the risk of resources being pulled from the project prematurely is low because this is a high-priority project to which CSM is strongly committed. Nonetheless, the assessment team argued that, in the past, they have seen too many instances when team members were pulled from an "important project"—so they still felt this concern remained

TABLE 2-2 B2B Project Risk Level Assessments

Risks	Team-Identified Impact	Executives' Tolerance
Technology constraint—getting software, hardware, partnered license	High	High
Pulling resources prematurely	High	Medium
Facility limitation	Low	Low
Availability of networking	Low	Low
Organizational constraints—people being pulled away for other projects	High	Low
Customer constraint—availability of customer to do connectivity, customer shelving the project	High	High

a high risk. The two teams reached a consensus that the issue of not pulling resources from the project needs would be mentioned in the charter.

Project Leadership Considerations

Risk assessment should start with the key project participants who are already assigned identifying the different potential sources of risk. These risks may include:

- Customer-associated
- Contract
- Project requirements
- Business practice expertise
- Project management
- Work estimates
- Project constraints
- Complexity and scale of deliverables
- Contractors.[1]

It is imperative that potential projects be assessed for risks by both management at a high level and technical experts at a detailed level. There are different schools of thought on the composition of assessment teams. Some argue that it is important to have a totally independent team make this assessment objectively and then play no other role on the project. Others argue that seamless transitions are preferable, and that those who will implement the project should be involved from the start. In an organization that values and trusts its associates and that attempts to maximize communications, we believe that the latter approach make more sense. Simultaneously, the executives involved should determine how much risk they are willing to tolerate for each identified category. Then the assessment team and the executives should together determine whether the risks appear to be acceptable.

Everyone needs to express their views candidly based upon their experience and expertise. In the end all parties must agree on the risk level in each category. Sometimes the project approach may need to be altered to reduce the risk levels in one or more areas to an acceptable level. The project leaders should ask themselves the following questions to determine if they are ready to proceed to their third responsibility, which is to justify and select the project:

- Can we develop a sense of shared risk with the project team, client, suppliers, and upper management?
- Have we started having useful discussions in identifying problems and approaches to solving them?

- Have we prepared for the worst while hoping for the best?
- Do we have the ability to identify risks soon enough to overcome them?
- Are we consciously trying to understand who gives us good vs. bad advice?
- Are we identifying opportunities along with risks?
- Have we assessed risk using the categories shown above?

It is clear that in the B2B project we are using as an example, both executives and the assessment team met to assess project risks. What is not as clear is whether they were thorough enough to ensure that all potential sources of risk were considered. A wise project leader really explores the details when assessing risks. Many things look fine on the surface, but trouble lies buried beneath. Leaders want to find that trouble early enough to handle it.

Project Leadership Lesson: Initiating—Project Details
A Project Leader Needs to:
Accept necessary project risks
Have the courage to challenge risks that can be mitigated
Exercise the wisdom to understand the difference between these two types of risk.

JUSTIFY AND SELECT THE PROJECT

After considering a variety of options, the team narrowed them to two possible approaches. The first approach was to implement the order processing and shipping module of the ERP system and use the software provided by the customer to automate the process. The other approach was to implement the software provided by the customer to automate the process within its existing legacy system.

The next step was to perform a cost benefit analysis of both options. This is shown in Table 2-3.

The team selected the first option. This option was determined to be the superior solution in that it contained all the benefits of process automation, was relatively quick with the customer-supplied software, and gave the company a foothold into the ERP system, which it would need to start implementing within a year anyway.

Project Leadership Considerations

Project selection is similar whether a company is selecting one project or a portfolio of projects. Project leaders need to be able to articulate the busi-

TABLE 2-3 Potential Project Cost Benefit Overview

Solution Proposed	Cost Components Related to Project	Benefits
Implement order processing and shipping module of ERP system and use the software provided by the customer	Resource costs Training costs (Software and hardware costs already budgeted under IT)	• Better visibility into the supply chain, reduced cycle time, inventory and inventory-related costs, seamless integration with customers, lays foundation for later to extend it to WIP, production schedules etc. • Interfacing with the new system, which would be implemented over a time frame of one year and is going to integrate all their diverse systems
Implement the software provided by the customer with their legacy system	Resource costs	• Better visibility into the supply chain, reduced cycle time, inventory and inventory-related costs, seamless integration with their customers, lays foundation for later to extend it to WIP, production schedules etc.

ness case for a potential project so that all key stakeholders can understand its value. In this situation, the project aligned so well with CSM's mission that selection was almost a given. The more interesting decision in this project selection was which approach to take. CSM was appropriate in first considering several potential solutions and then looking hard at the last two when the others did not appear feasible.

This same approach can be used when there are many more potential choices. First a team needs to brainstorm all the potential approaches (which can sometimes be numerous). Each participant should feel free to offer any approach without fear that it will be criticized. This is important since some ideas that first appear impractical may later prove to be worthwhile. Moreover, this sets the tone for free and open discussion on the project.

Once all potential approaches are listed, the team needs to have a method of quickly screening a large number of choices down to a small number that can be analyzed in detail. Sometimes project participants perform this screening by asking questions about which approaches are not feasible. If there are quite a few choices to be considered, a second method worth considering is multi-voting. In multi-voting each participant can vote for whichever approaches he or she prefers. The group then progressively removes first the really impractical approaches and then the practical but not quite ideal approaches. A key to multi-voting is to try not to remove more than half of the potential approaches at one time, which can result in good choices being removed along with impractical ones.

Once there are few enough potential approaches left that it is practical to perform detailed analysis, each alternative should be examined based on relevant dimensions. The dimensions that are often considered include:

- Strategic and/or commercial value
- Risk
- Stability of requirements
- Competition
- Opportunities for learning
- Fit in the portfolio of current projects
- Expected duration
- Cost
- Resource needs
- Leadership needs
- Training needs.

Before committing to a project, a company might use four different frames of leadership (political, human resources, traditional management, and symbolic) as lenses through which to view the project. Certainly an ethics check is necessary for all projects. A look at the broad picture or external environment is also necessary: Are there political, economic, or social issues? An internal look at the project's impact on the development of resources and relationships between and among all stakeholders is also important: How does the project build expertise for associates? What impact will it have on suppliers? Regulators? Other customers? Competitors? It appears that none of these factors is an issue in this case.

Project Leadership Lesson: Initiating—Project Integration

A Project Leader Needs to:

Consider different potential projects or approaches based solely on their merits

Have the courage to accept or reject projects and approaches based on their merits

Exercise the wisdom to make the right choices.

SELECT KEY PROJECT PARTICIPANTS

Mark asked his executive team to select a project sponsor. The team agreed that Gary and Bob are the two strongest candidates. Profiles of each are shown in Table 2-4.

The executive team decided to select Bob as the project sponsor. They also created a steering team of Bob, Carl, Gary, Mark, and Peter.

TABLE 2-4 Profiles of Potential Sponsors

Bob's Profile	Gary's Profile
Participative leadership style	Technology initiator
Aware of organizational politics within the functional organizations	Understands supply chain inefficiencies
Results-oriented	Believes in ROI of IT projects
Great communicator	Likes outdoor sports
Factual and thoroughly works out details	Experience in being project sponsor

Bob mentioned to Gary that there were two possible candidates for the job of project manager. The qualifications of both candidates are shown in Table 2-5.

Bob told Gary that he needed someone who was confident, enthusiastic, logical, and who finds flaws in advance. After meeting with both candidates, Bob selected Uma as the project manager.

Bob and Uma selected the core team as shown in Table 2-6.

TABLE 2-5 Project Manager Candidate Qualifications

Qualifications	Jack Donovan	Uma Raman
Job Title	Manager of business applications	IT project manager
Education	Degree in engineering	Masters in computer science, MBA, PMP
PM experience	10 years	5 years
Last Project	Selected ERP system for CSM	Global project in an Internet company
Supervisor's Comments	Task-oriented, micromanages work breakdown structure (WBS), honesty, integrity, technically up-to-date.	Strong interpersonal skills, great problem-solving capabilities, aggressive, has fun days in her project

TABLE 2-6 Core Team Members and Roles

Team Member	Functional Role
Jeff Gardiner	Southeastern regional sales director
Steve Alvarez	Procurement manager
Rob Richard	Responsible for advanced shipping notices
Rita Elliot	Accounts receivable manager
Scott Brown	Networking manager
Elizabeth Ramsey	Operations manager
Paul Byrant	QA manager
Sanjay Krishnan	Technical lead
Chris Chin	Lead business analyst

Project Leadership Considerations

A large part of the success of any project is determined at this point. In choosing key participants, the first goal is to find people who have adequate knowledge and skills in team-building, planning, communications, and decision-making to be effective project leaders. Appendix B is a self-scoring assessment of an individual's project leadership potential. The key project leaders selected should in turn find people who will have a synergy among them, that is, who will work creatively together and whose efforts will complement and supplement each other. Key project participants typically include a steering team, project sponsor, project manager, project core team, and subject matter experts.

The steering team needs to include people of vision who see the project in perspective, who care about the project's success, and who will provide overall guidance and support for the project. In some instances the organization's existing management team serves this function. An advantage of this approach is that the steering team by definition has legitimate authority (clout). In other instances individuals are specifically selected to serve on the project steering team. An advantage of this approach is that the steering team may have more specific expertise and passion. CSM elected to select the steering team.

The sponsor is usually a member of the steering team and is the primary liaison between the steering team and the project, although many informal lines of communication may also exist between the steering team and the project. The sponsor is primarily responsible for securing resources, removing obstacles, and mentoring the project manager and the core team.

Bob appears to be a wise choice for sponsor since he understands organizations, communicates well, and works effectively with teams. While Bob's technical expertise appears weaker than Gary's, other participants can provide expertise. In a true team setting, the experts will lead within their competence. Bob's willingness to ask detailed questions should help.

The project manager is the primary communicator both internally within the project and externally with many individuals and groups who have an interest in the project. When situations call for action, the project manager needs to be able to:
- Advocate a project vision effectively
- Keep attention focused on key issues
- Listen well and speak clearly
- Inspire confidence

- Create a sense of urgency
- Care for and protect people
- Defend the core values of the organization and project
- Lead change fearlessly
- Coordinate a multitude of tasks
- Make sensible tradeoff decisions.

Uma appears to be a good choice. Since the two key people have been chosen, it is now time for Uma (the project manager) to assess herself and Bob (the project sponsor) in terms of their personality types, their emotional intelligence, their team-building skills, their weaknesses, and their professional needs and desires. The project manager and sponsor will need to communicate effectively with many people, including the steering team, who will guide them, and the project core team, who will collectively make many project decisions and perform many of the project's tasks.

A project core team is generally a small group of people who are assigned to the project during initiating and remain for the duration. They collectively make many project decisions and either perform or lead the performance of most of the project tasks. Bob and Uma decided that subject matter experts (SMEs) would not be members of the core team, but would be selected on a just-in-time basis.

Project core team members then need to be chosen based upon three general criteria: their technical competence, their ability to help the team function well, and their desire to do whatever it takes to complete the project successfully. This is a good situation for Uma. Since she is choosing several people at once and the positional leaders are known, she can balance her choices, perhaps accepting someone with a technical competence that is hard to find who lacks certain teaming skills and finding another person with those skills. Diversity is the key: She will want to choose people with different styles, experiences, and approaches to problem-solving to ensure that many possibilities are considered.

The project core team needs to comprise committed, qualified, and diverse people. It is wise to have a mix of very experienced individuals and some new players who can learn and be developed during this process. Bob and the steering team need to ensure that Uma sees the bigger picture and chooses people who will be effective in this project and in future projects. It does appear that a wide range of departments is represented on the project.

One key question to ask when deciding if someone should be on the core team is: Do we need this person's expertise throughout the project or just part of the time? The core team ideally should remain intact for the entire project.

Another key question is how big the core team should be. While many factors enter into this decision, one useful rule of thumb is that smaller teams communicate more easily. An offsetting factor is that different departments and units need to be represented when decisions are made.

The last major role is for SMEs. These individuals are brought onto the project as needed, and some may perform a little work on many projects. One challenge with SMEs is to get them to buy into the project. Since they have less involvement, often they have less commitment. While many SMEs are selected just-in-time, some critical resources are in such short supply that the need for their services should be identified and prioritized as far in advance as possible.

Project Leadership Lesson: Initiating—Human Resources

A Project Leader Needs to:

Accept the weaknesses and idiosyncracies of potential key project participants

Have the courage to select appropriate participants and reject inappropriate participants

Exercise the wisdom to make the right choices.

DETERMINE TEAM OPERATING METHODS

Bob, Uma, and the team gathered in the conference room. Bob invited Gary from the steering team to join them. Bob welcomed the group and introduced the steering team and the core team. Bob and Gary made the same presentation they gave to the executive team highlighting the importance of this project. Gary told them that the first task would be to come up with a couple of potential approaches and a project charter. Uma then addressed the team and said "I welcome you all. I hope that you all understand why you are part of this team. I am looking forward to working with you. Expect to be in meetings for the next couple of days." As soon as she said that, Jeff started thinking that he would rather be out in the field selling and earning commissions instead of being stuck in meetings.

Uma sensed that the group might have questions about her, since not many of them had worked with her before. After the meeting Scott mentioned to Paul that the last time he had a woman project manager she was very emotional and controlling.

Uma decided to have the first meeting in an informal atmosphere at a park nearby where lunch would be served. She hoped that the offsite meeting would help the team get to know each other in an informal setting. When they all gathered at the park Uma welcomed each one of them, mentioning that all of them bring value to the team and that each is very important to the team. Uma asked each team member to introduce themselves and say what they like to do for fun. She also asked them to share their good and bad experiences on their previous projects and ask any questions they had about her.

After everyone introduced themselves, the team started dispersing into small groups. By the end of the day Scott thought that he should not compare Uma with his last woman project manager but should judge her on her own merits. Jeff, who had been very apprehensive, was having fun and enjoying the company of Elizabeth.

The next morning the entire team (including Bob, the sponsor) met in the conference room. The day's agenda was to develop a team mission, identify roles and responsibilities, develop team operating methods, and formalize decision-making procedures. Bob quoted Stephen Covey: "An empowering organizational mission statement focuses on contribution, on worthwhile purposes that create a collective deep burning 'Yes!' . . . It contains both vision and principle-based values. It addresses the needs of the stakeholder."[2] He also said that the team has to deal with the five basic elements of desired results, guidelines, resources, accountability, and consequences.

Elizabeth stated, "In my last project, for each meeting we would assign a facilitator and a scribe. When the project manager could not attend, we assigned someone else to lead the meetings." The team thought it was a good idea. Bob volunteered to be the facilitator and Elizabeth to serve as the scribe for this meeting.

After the mission was determined, Uma asked the team to discuss team operating methods and decision-making procedures. Paul said he had found team charters useful in the past and suggested they develop their own team charter to supplement the project charter. The team, however, decided to incorporate team methods into the project charter.

Project Leadership Considerations

By using an inviting approach, it appears that Uma has broken down many prejudices and assumptions and helped each team member get excited about her, the project, and other team members. It is important to establish a climate of openness, trust, and fun. This climate must recognize that individuals have different needs, concerns, and abilities to change. The project leader should honor each individual while establishing workable team operating methods. Appendix C is a project leadership assessment that can be used both now, while project team operating methods are being established, and during the project execution stage, when the project team is accomplishing its work.

The project's parent organization may strongly influence the operating methods. At the more formalized end of the spectrum, some organizations have quite specific operating methods that all project teams are expected to follow. Organizations like these often have reminders mounted in conference rooms, templates in shared network files, trained facilitators to help new teams, and other measures to ensure that all project teams follow the prescribed operating methods. At the less formalized end, some organizations not only have no standards, but also have little patience for project teams that want to take time up front to establish operating methods. Many organizations fall somewhere between the extremes.

The reasons for having project team operating methods is to prevent some problems from occurring in the first place, smooth out difficulties, help the team use their time efficiently, and create an atmosphere for making decisions that minimize inappropriate conflict. Some of the more frequently developed operating methods include decision-making and meeting management.

Decision-Making

Several types of decision-making are useful in projects: consensus, leader-imposed, delegated, voting, and scoring models. Each method has its place. A wise leader learns when each is desirable and how to facilitate each decision-making method.

True consensus occurs when every person on the project team agrees that the decision makes sense and he or she will enthusiastically support it. Each project team member must be committed to supporting the decision even when it may not be his or her personal favorite. Achieving true consensus takes time, effort, and deep understanding of all the underlying issues (not just the stated positions) in a situation. Consensus should be used primarily when enthusiastic buy-in will be needed to implement a critical project decision.

Some project decisions must conform to organizational desires. When this is the case, leaders—especially the sponsor and the project manager—should make the decision and inform the team. Project leaders can also make many minor decisions.

A wise project leader, however, will delegate many of the minor decisions. This delegation accomplishes several desired outcomes. First, it unburdens the project leader, freeing him or her to spend more time and energy on issues that are important at the leader's level. Second, it can be very empowering to project team members to make more of their own decisions. Third, especially if the decision involves technical details, a team member may be able to make a better decision. Delegating progressively more important decisions is a process in which the team member demonstrates an increasing ability to make sound decisions and the project leader actively mentors the team member. This delegation process is one of the important skills effective project leaders must develop.

Voting can be used in several ways. First, multi-voting can be used by a project team to quickly screen a large list of potential options to a manageable number of options that can be considered in more detail. Informal polling is sometimes useful when testing for consensus. In that sense, it can be part of the consensus development. Voting should rarely be used, however, for making final decisions because losers in the voting will probably not be enthusiastic supporters of the decision.

Scoring models, sometimes called weighted scoring models or prioritization matrixes, are useful when multiple criteria—some of which are more important than others—need to be considered. For example, before buying a car most people will consider several factors, such as cost, gas mileage, and style, and will weigh them differently. The scoring models are a formalized method for teams to make these kinds of decisions. A scoring model example is shown in Table 2-7.

When using a scoring model, the project team should:

1. *Decide what criteria are important* in the upcoming decision. In the example shown in Table 2-7, cost, schedule, risk, and buy-in were selected. (Cost and schedule are usually quantitative while buy-in is an example of a subjective criterion for which the group will need to decide on the rating.)

2. *"Weight" the importance of each criterion.* This is easily accomplished by deciding which criterion is most important and then determining the comparative importance of each of the other criteria. Sometimes

TABLE 2-7 Scoring Model

Alternative Approaches	Cost (20%)	Schedule (10%)	Technical Risk (30%)	Buy-in (40%)	Total Score
A	1 (.2)	5 (.5)	2 (.6)	2 (.8)	2.1
B	3 (.6)	3 (.3)	3 (.9)	1 (.4)	2.2
C	5 (1.0)	3 (.3)	5 (1.5)	4 (1.6)	4.4

a project sponsor will complete these first two steps to ensure that the decision supports what he or she feels is important. In this example, the criteria importance weights add up to 100 percent. Buy-in was determined to be the most important, followed by risk, cost, and then schedule. There can be a tie in importance—for example, cost and risk could both have been 25 percent.

3. *Generate a list of alternatives.* This is best accomplished after the criteria have been established and weighted since there is less temptation to manipulate the process at this point. These are shown as approaches A, B, and C.

4. *Rate each alternative on each criterion.* This is most easily accomplished if the team uses a simple scale of 1 to 5 (with 5 being the best). The project team should rate all alternatives on one criterion before moving to the second criterion. In this example, all three approaches should have been rated on cost before any other criterion is considered. Also, in this example note that Alternative C was rated 5, meaning it was the best, B was rated 3, meaning average, and C was rated 1, meaning worst.

5. *Multiply the rating times the weight for each cell* (that is, for each alternative on each criterion). For example, the cost cell on alternative B was rated 3 and worth a weighting of .2, for a weighted score of .6.

6. *Add across the rows to get a total score for each alternative.* The one with the highest weighted score wins.

Meeting Management

The project team will spend a great deal of time in meetings. Therefore, it is sensible to establish a meeting process and to work continuously to improve this process. This includes:

- Creating and distributing advance agendas
- Delineating roles such as leader, facilitator, and scribe
- Recording and sharing useful meeting minutes
- Evaluating the meeting process with an eye toward improvement
- Completing agreed-upon tasks between meetings.

A project leader who would like to improve the meeting process can use the plan, do, check, act model[3] to illustrate the process, as shown in Figure 2-1.

An agenda should be created and sent to the project team members before each meeting so they can be prepared for the meeting. Agendas are often also

---

FIGURE 2-1   The Meeting Cycle

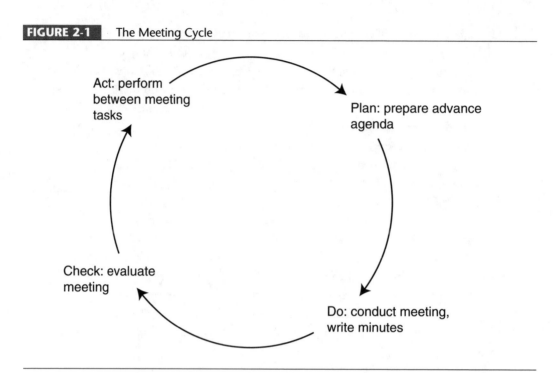

Act: perform between meeting tasks

Plan: prepare advance agenda

Check: evaluate meeting

Do: conduct meeting, write minutes

---

posted in shared folders or on intranets or otherwise distributed so other key project stakeholders are aware of what will be discussed at upcoming meetings. Figure 2-2 presents a meeting agenda template.

Bob and Uma were appropriate in performing the facilitator and scribe roles at the first core team meeting. As leaders it is wise to role-model behavior before insisting that others perform in the same fashion. To help the core team develop, both as individuals and as a team, Bob and Uma should set the expectation that other team members will serve as facilitator and scribe in future meetings.

Effective project teams also record important information shared, decisions made, upcoming issues identified, action items committed to, and improvements suggested in terse but accurate minutes. Figure 2-3 provides an example of a meeting minutes template.

A wise project leader will take a couple of minutes at the end of a project meeting to ask what went well at this meeting that we would like to repeat and what could be improved. A simple technique to capture this information is called "plus delta," with *plus* representing positive items and *delta* representing items to be changed. It is important for a leader to respond to every sugges-

FIGURE 2-2   Meeting Agenda

Team _____	Date _____	Time _____	Place _____

PURPOSE: _____

Topic	Person	Outcomes	Time
Review agenda	_____	Understanding	2 min
_____	_____	_____	_____
_____	_____	_____	_____
_____	_____	_____	_____
Summary	_____	Agreement	5 min
Meeting evaluation	_____	Improvement	2 min

tion and to follow up to ensure that helpful suggestions are implemented. The discerning project leader will develop a feel for how to respond to each suggestion. When conducting a plus delta evaluation, the project leader will usually use a flip chart or marker board to have it visible, but then have the scribe copy the results in the project team minutes.

The final part of project meeting management is the work team members do in between meetings. Good project leaders develop a sense for what kind of conversations to have with each team member to ensure that their work is completed correctly and on time, but without overmanaging capable and willing workers.

Project Leadership Lesson: Initiating—Human Relations

A Project Leader Needs to:

Accept that individuals have needs that must be honored

Have the courage to develop project team operating methods that must be followed

Exercise the wisdom to know when each is appropriate.

FIGURE 2-3 Meeting Minutes

Team _____	Date _____	Time _____	Place _____
Members Present:			
Information Shared:			
Decisions Made:			
Issues:			

Action Item	Person Responsible	Completion Date
Meeting Evaluation		

DEVELOP TOP MANAGEMENT SUPPORT

At this point Bob and Uma went before the steering team. Uma talked with passion about the project, highlighting how it was going to help build customer relationships. She did a good job convincing Mark and Gary. Peter raised the question, "Why is this project more important than a new research and development initiative which is being pushed to the next quarter?" Uma answered him, saying that this B2B project is important to our existing customers and is in alignment with our business philosophy of partnering with customers. Peter's department (engineering) will gain help in automating the transfer of engineering drawings and expediting production schedules. Mark as CEO added his comments and vision for the future of the company and indicated that he felt that the project should be approved. At that point everyone on the executive team agreed.

Project Leadership Considerations

What we have observed in Bob and Uma's meeting with the steering team is the culmination of an ongoing dialogue. It appears they have done a good job in laying the groundwork for top management support of their B2B project. The approval came quickly at this point, indicating that there was probably informal communication with the key leaders prior to this meeting. Uma's skillful handling of Peter's question, showing him how his department would benefit, left him no option but to agree and diffused his criticism. Possibly Peter's question suggests that Bob and Uma may not have informally answered all of his concerns in advance. While project leaders try to head off problems, frequently a few questions remain.

Wise project leaders will open multiple informal channels of communication and keep them open. One key lesson is: Never surprise your boss. It is prudent for a project leader to think of the entire steering team as multiple bosses. While open communication is generally a good idea with supporters, there may be one or two members of the steering team who are so antagonistic to a particular approach that convincing evidence should be developed before communicating with them.

Developing top management support is vital since any senior executive who is hostile to a project may find a way to sabotage it. A project manager does not want a difficult project to be accepted by a vote of five executives for it and four executives against it.

Project managers often need to coordinate the efforts of various workers from different disciplines over whom they have no authority. While this may be challenging it is often a reality in modern leadership—and is also a helpful experience for moving up in the leadership ranks in an organization. The exposure that project managers have in developing top management support provides an excellent opportunity to develop their leadership skills and stature within an organization. Junior project managers should see this wooing of top management support as an opportunity for visibility and should make every effort to perform this responsibility well, both for the immediate sake of their project and for the long-term sake of their career.

Project Leadership Lesson: Initiating—Project Promotion
A Project Leader Needs to:
Accept the true concerns of various top managers in the parent organization
Have the courage to challenge top managers' concerns that are the result of narrow or biased thinking
Exercise the wisdom to know the difference between these two types of concerns.

COMMIT TO THE PROJECT

Bob and Uma took the project charter that had been approved by the steering team back to the project core team for a signing ceremony. The steering team also recommended an incentive of 10 percent of salary for the successful on-budget, on-time completion of this vital project. Everyone enjoyed refreshments as they celebrated the successful close of the project initiating stage and prepared for the project planning stage. The project charter is shown in Figure 2-4.

Project Leadership Considerations

The initiating stage of a project is complete when the project team and the sponsor sign the charter. The charter is one of the most important project documents and, arguably, the one that project sponsors have the most personal involvement in creating. Project sponsors must ensure that other planning and control documents are completed, but they must be personally involved in the creation of a charter. Other project leaders (that is, the project manager and the core team members) will have extensive personal involvement in creating other planning and control documents in addition to the charter.

A project charter is a contract between the project core team and the sponsor (who represents both senior management of the organization and the outside customer). As with a contract, the people who sign the charter should ensure that they understand and agree to every detail within it. Either party (the sponsor or the project core team) can write the rough draft and then very candidly discuss each part of the charter with the other party. Sometimes the sponsor tells the core team right at the start which items are especially important, but more often either the team creates the rough draft or both parties develop it together. When both parties work together, the session is often facilitated by either an outside consultant or a disinterested executive from the parent organization (that is, one whose own area will not be substantially impacted by the project). Many organizations understand that serving as a project facilitator is a learning experience for rising executives and choose to assign this role to managers who show promise.

Essentially, a charter has two purposes. First, everyone involved in the upcoming project needs to develop a common understanding of what the project is all about. Second, each person needs to personally and formally commit to doing their best to achieve the agreed-upon project results—even when things do not go as planned. Many organizations have developed their

FIGURE 2-4   B2B Project Charter

Project Purpose:
The expectations of the project are to implement the order processing and shipping module of the ERP system and to implement the software provided by their customer Buslog to enable seamless integration of order processing between the two companies. The business purposes of the project are better visibility into the supply chain, reduced cycle time, reduction of inventory costs, and seamless integration with our customers.

Deliverables
The project team will produce the following deliverables for review:
• Statement of work, including resource plan and preliminary schedule
• System design specification
• Technical design (Including architecture, technical design, network design, map specifications, and test plans)
• Developed and configured system (includes development, configuration, network setup, and internal integration testing)
• Validated system (system acceptance testing, including end-to-end testing with partner)
• Validated transition document.

Milestone Schedule

Phase	Duration
Project Initiating and Planning	3 weeks
Requirements Analysis/ Systems Design and Architecture	3 weeks
Technical and Network Design	2 weeks
Technical Development and Configuration/ Network Configuration	8 weeks
System Acceptance Testing	3 weeks
Transition and Transition Support	2 weeks

Budget
The initial budget approved for this project is $7 million. The budget covers the resource cost and any additional costs required. The software and hardware costs have already been approved under the IT budget and are not included in the project budget.

Risks

Risks	Impact
Technology constraint—getting software, hardware, partnered license	High
Resource constraint	High
Facility limitation	Low
Availability of networking	Low
Organizational constraints—people being pulled away for other projects	Medium—based on commitment from steering committee
Customer constraint—availability of customer to do connectivity, customer shelving the project	High

Out of Scope
The implementation of other modules of the ERP system and automating other business transactions with the customer are out-of-scope.

Team Operating Principles
       • Team members will trust one another.
       • Team members will be 100% committed to the project.
       • Team members will share ideas, communicate, and listen.
       • All team members are empowered to make decisions within their areas of expertise.
       • Decisions may be delegated, made by consensus, or made by the project manager as decided by the team.
       • The team will track progress.

Roles and Responsibilities

Name	Signature and Date	Name	Signature and Date
Bob McCally, Project Sponsor		Uma Raman, Project Manager	
Steve Alvarez		Scott Brown	
Paul Bryant		Chris Chin	
Jeff Gardiner		Rob Richard	
Rita Elliot		Elizabeth Ramsey	
Sanjay Krishnan			

own ideas of what must be included in a charter to accomplish these two goals. Organizations value speed and simplicity when creating charters. The charter is written to get a quick understanding of what is involved in completing the potential project with the knowledge that, if something is not acceptable, the project may not get approved. In many organizations projects are not considered official until a charter is completed and signed.

Listed below are some of the typical key sections that are included in a project charter. For ease of remembering, we present these sections as the three "W"s to be accomplished, subject to the three "H"s, by using the three "C"s. We briefly define each section and list popular alternative names. Note that while the intent of most of these sections is included in many charters, many organizations combine sections or leave out one or two. As long as the two purposes of the charter (agreement and commitment) are accomplished, the exact format is certainly negotiable.

Typical Elements of a Charter

- The Three Ws:
  - **Why**—also known as mission, purpose, objectives, or business case. This is the reason for undertaking the project. It is hard to commit to something unless you understand why it is important.
  - **What**—also known as scope overview or deliverables. This describes what will be accomplished.
  - **When**—also known as milestone schedule. This lists when key portions of this project should be completed. Critical success factors or metrics are a brief listing of what should be monitored closely to ensure that the project is making adequate progress; they are often the basis for the milestone schedule.
- The Three Hs:
  - **How much**—also known as budget or spending authority. This shows how much the project is expected to cost and may include limits on specific aspects.
  - **Hazards**—also known as risks and assumptions. This identifies what might go wrong, how likely each risk is, the consequences if the risk happens, and what the project team plans to do about each risk.
  - **How**—also known as team operating principles or methods. This describes how the team will function. Organizations often have this established for all project teams and incorporate it by reference.

- The Three Cs:
  - **Communication plan**—also known as reviews, approvals, and reports. This describes who needs to know what information, when, and in what format.
  - **Collection of knowledge**—also known as lessons learned and lessons shared or post mortems. This describes how this project team will perform this project better based upon what they learned from at least one previous project. A wise sponsor will not sign a charter until the project team has convinced her that they have learned from studying previous projects.
  - **Commitment**—also known as signature block or roles and responsibilities. This lists who is involved and often describes the extent to which each person can make decisions. It also is how the project team members publicly and personally show their commitment to the project by signing the charter.

The B2B team did the most important thing by constructing the charter that each team member and the sponsor representing top management publicly signed. The charter is pretty good as far as it goes.

The purpose statement includes two of the Ws: what and why. The deliverables expand on the what and the milestone schedule addresses the last W: when.

The three Hs are also covered, but are not very complete. The budget is how much (although it often must have more detail and support). The risks are the hazards. While these are listed, having three high-risk items should raise come concerns about the project approach. Team operating principles (the how) such as "team members will trust each other" seem pretty simplistic and hard to enforce.

Notably missing are most of the Cs. Commitment is the most important C and that is included in the roles and responsibilities. However, the communication plan and the collection of knowledge are entirely missing. Collection of knowledge (lessons learned and shared) will help a project team make better plans based upon the successes and mistakes of previous projects. These lessons learned should also be in the charter. Project teams often put the communication plan off until the planning stage. That is also acceptable—as long as it is accomplished. It is very important to remember who needs project information, when, and in what format, and then to provide that information. When people do not have the information they need, they are likely to guess and the rumors they spread will frequently cause problems for a project. A wise project leader will try to balance the needs for these W, H, and C elements for their charter with their interest in keeping things simple and keeping them moving.

Project Leadership Lesson: Initiating—Commitment
A Project Leader Needs to:
Accept his or her responsibilities as a project leader
Have the courage to help other project participants accept their responsibilities
Exercise the wisdom to understand the difference between these two types of responsibility.

Now that the charter is approved, the project team is ready to move into detailed project planning. The role of senior project leaders (sponsors) may diminish somewhat as they oversee the details rather than plan them personally; the role of the junior project leaders (all others) remains high during planning. Depending on the needs of each project, the amount of time that project leaders need to personally spend will sometimes diminish during project execution and closing.

NOTES

1. Paul S. Royer, *Project Risk Management: A Proactive Approach* (Vienna, VA: Management Concepts, Inc., 2002), p. 18.
2. Stephen R. Covey *et al.*, *First Things First* (New York: Simon & Schuster, 1994), p. 222.
3. Timothy J. Kloppenborg and Joseph A. Petrick, "Meeting Management and Group Character Development," *Journal of Managerial Issues* 11, no. 2 (1999), 166-179.

CHAPTER 3

Project Planning

Project planning is the second of the four stages in the project lifecycle model (as highlighted in Table 3-1). This is when detailed planning of the project is completed. During this stage of the project lifecycle, the scope, activities, resources, communications, and budget are planned. Large, complex, unfamiliar projects will require more in-depth planning than small, simple, and familiar projects. Depending on the size of the core team, different subteams may plan details and then the core team will integrate all the individual sections to create a complete project plan.

TABLE 3-1   Project Leader Responsibilities: Planning

Category of Project Leadership Task	Project Leadership Stage			
	Initiating	**Planning**	**Executing**	**Closing**
Project Priorities	Align project with parent organization	Understand and respond to the customer	Authorize work	Audit project
Project Details	Perform risk analysis	Oversee detailed plan development	Monitor progress and control changes	Terminate project
Project Integration	Justify and select project	Integrate project plans	Coordinate work across multiple projects	Capture and share lessons learned
Human Resources	Select key project participants	Select remainder of project participants	Supervise work performance	Reassign workers
Human Relations	Determine team operating methods	Develop team communications plan	Lead teams	Reward and recognize participants
Project Promotion	Develop top management support	Motivate all participants	Maintain morale	Celebrate project completion
Project Commitment	Commit to project	Secure key stakeholder approval	Secure customer acceptance	Oversee administrative closure

Regardless of the size and complexities of the project, all projects share common project leadership tasks during project planning. These include:
- Understand and respond to the customer
- Oversee detailed plan development
- Integrate the overall project plan
- Select remainder of project participants
- Develop communications plan
- Motivate all participants
- Secure stakeholder approval.

UNDERSTAND AND RESPOND TO THE CUSTOMER

As the CSM project manager, Uma felt that some of the team members were concerned that they did not know all the requirements of the project. Since Uma had not yet initiated conversation with her counterpart at Buslog Technologies, she asked Bob, as the CSM project sponsor, to schedule a meeting of the project core teams at Buslog and CSM. Bob arranged for a conference call with Terry Andrews, project sponsor, Cecil Jones, project manager, and the other key people from Buslog.

Bob facilitated the call and introduced everyone. He conveyed to Buslog that CSM is committed to working with them to make the project successful. He also mentioned that the interface between the two companies would start in a couple of months, after CSM completed its project plan. Bob mentioned that the CSM project team would like to work with Buslog to create the project plan for the B2B implementation. Terry concurred. Bob explained that the purpose of this meeting was to understand the customer's high-level needs. Various Buslog people discussed their expectations. After the call the CSM core team felt that they generally understood the needs of the people within the customer organization.

Uma facilitated the meeting, using the supplier-input-process-output-customer (SIPOC) model to identify customer needs. She explained that the SIPOC is a tool that can be used to improve the project process by clearly identifying relationships among suppliers, inputs, processes, outputs, and customers. She said that they would work backwards from the customer's needs. They identified the needs of Buslog and then the internal stakeholders for the order processing system. The B2B project SIPOC model is shown in Figure 3-1.

The team thought that this would provide them the input they needed for the scope definition. Since an error in a single transaction could cost millions of dollars, there could be no compromise in the quality of the B2B system.

FIGURE 3-1	B2B Project Supplier-Input-Process-Output-Customers (SIPOC) Model

Supplier	Input	Process	Output	Customer
Functional team members in the project team and additional stakeholders Technical team (IT) and business team leads Operations team Buslog Technologies	Existing process flow of business internally to CSM purchase order processing and ASN process between CSM and Buslog Internal process flow between Shipping and Accounting Hardware and software involved Document used Standards used New hardware, software	Start → Planning–Statement of work → System/architecture design → Technical design → Development and configuration → Integration testing → External integration testing → System acceptance → User training → Transition and closure → Stop	• System design specification document • Technical design document • Developed, configured, and validated order processing system • Validated transition document • Working business-to-business system between CSM and Buslog • User training • Other deliverables	Buslog Technologies Order processing Shipping Accounting Purchasing

Bob began by setting the priorities for the team. He told the group that quality could not be traded off. Cost could be traded off only if the steering committee approved.

Uma had another conversation with her counterpart Cecil to get more specific inputs on project priorities. Cecil mentioned that the go-live date is a hard one and Buslog can't compromise on that. From his perspective, the only thing they can trade off is the scope of the project.

Project Leadership Considerations

Documentation is needed for all meetings, both internal and external, and everyone needs a chance to respond to and correct errors or misunderstandings.

There are several aspects to understanding and responding to the customer, and this project team did a good job on most of them. First, the team needs to understand who the various customer groups are. The SIPOC model is very useful for this task. Working backward from the identification of all the customer groups, the core team can discover much useful planning information regarding customer needs. The SIPOC model should also serve as a starting point in the prioritization process.

Typically, a project is planned assuming that if everything goes right, the project team can successfully deliver all four customer priorities: the full project scope, on the agreed-upon schedule, at the agreed-upon cost, with the agreed-upon quality. However, on most projects unexpected things happen that either allow a project team to improve upon one or more of these four customer priorities or prevent the full attainment of one or more of these priorities. The project leaders should have frank discussions with the key customer groups (often this means both the external paying customer and one or more key internal stakeholders within the parent organization). The focus of these discussions needs to be which of the customer priorities take precedence.

For example, if things are going very well, should the project team try to lower cost, speed up the schedule, add more features to the project scope, or improve the quality of the project deliverables? The same understanding must be developed if things go poorly: Which of the customer priorities can be compromised and by how much? Many customers will tell a project leader that all four must be achieved. The wise project leader should respond that if all goes according to plan, that will happen, but as a responsible leader, she wants to make the same kind of decisions the customer himself would make if he were on the jobsite every day.

One area in which the project team could have done a better job is in documenting the conversations with the customer. In Chapter 2, simple minutes forms were introduced for use in project meetings. The intent of these minutes is to capture important information shared, decisions made, upcoming issues identified, commitments agreed to, and a meeting evaluation. The same type of information is appropriate to capture from other kinds of customer contacts such as conversations. After a conversation with a customer, a simple email to the customer confirming this information can be sent and a copy kept as project documentation.

Whenever possible, the first meeting with the project customers should be in person. Much of communication is reading and interpreting body language, and this is not possible by phone. A videoconference might be a useful compromise. Also, it is often wise to have a first meeting with the senior players: the project sponsors and managers from both companies. It may well make sense later on for members of the project teams to talk with each other directly, but a phone conversation with seven plus people is not an ideal way to start.

Project Leadership Lesson: Planning—Project Priorities

A Project Leader Needs to:

Accept that the customer has multiple, often conflicting wants

Have the courage to prioritize the customer's true needs

Exercise the wisdom to understand the difference between wants and needs.

OVERSEE DETAILED PLAN DEVELOPMENT

Uma reiterated to the team in a memo that they would use a lessons-learned process at every stage of the project. Uma wanted the team to brainstorm lessons learned from the planning stage of similar projects.

Sanjay realized that among the first tasks was choosing the hardware and software. Gary, as the CIO, needed to make these decisions. He also needed to select and hire consultants. However, this could not be accomplished until the schedule was developed.

Uma wanted the team to develop a risk plan detailing all the risks that were discussed in the initiation stage. This risk plan would include an assessment of the probability of each risk event happening, the consequences if it did happen, and contingency plans where needed. Some of the team members argued that they had already discussed the risk at the initiation stage and that was enough information for them to move forward with preparation of the work breakdown structure (WBS). She reminded the team that a WBS is a detailed listing of all the project work. They could include a contingency plan later in their schedule.

Uma sensed that the team was getting restless and wanted to get on with the project. She made it clear that she understood that some of the team members felt that they were not using time wisely, but she felt that time spent on risk planning was crucial. A mistake at this point could create a major problem later.

When the project charter was developed, the team had to develop time estimates for the major phases of the project. Now, as the team got ready to create the WBS, they decided the first step was to work on a major milestone plan and identify the deliverables at every milestone that would be shared with stakeholders for their approval. The milestone plan is shown in Table 3-2.

Having completed the major milestones, the core team began constructing the WBS. As they developed the WBS, they assigned resource requirements to every item. Estimated hours of resource requirements are summarized in Table 3-3.

Chris wanted more time allocated for design and Paul wanted more time allocated for quality assurance (QA). Uma then asked each of the team members to have a meeting with their subject matter experts (SMEs) separately to complete the WBS detail for their subteam's work. She also wanted them to show all dependencies and to input this into a schedule using Microsoft® Project. Then Uma took their individual schedules, merged all of them into a

TABLE 3-2 B2B Project Milestone Plan

Milestone	Delivery week	Deliverable
Project planning and initiation	Week 2	Project charter, project scope definition, work breakdown structure, project budget plan, communications plan
Requirements analysis, system design specification and architecture	Week 5	Systems requirements document, use case document, functional specifications, technical architecture design document
Technical design and network design	Week 7	Technical design specification document, network design document
Development and configuration	Week 15	Order processing system ready for integration testing, documentation of configuration, customized user manuals, training materials
System acceptance testing	Week 18	Test plans used for testing, results of regression testing
Training	Week 19	Training manuals
Transition and transition support	Week 21	Transition document detailing roles and responsibilities in the day-to-day maintenance of the system

TABLE 3-3 B2B Project Resource Requirements

WBS Category	Resource	Hours
Requirements analysis	Consultant	80
System design and architecture	Consultant	60
Technical and network design	Consultant	80
	Internal	160
Development	5 full-time internal 2 consultants	2000

schedule for the entire project, and presented it to the whole team, including the SMEs. After much discussion and various requests, a schedule emerged that everyone felt was reasonable.

Bob and Uma then used the schedule as input for their detailed budget. They broke down costs into the major components of internal resources, subcontractors, consultants, training, travel and administration, and cost of the project office. They assigned costs to major WBS components and decided to track actual costs against their estimates. Then Bob and Uma shared their results with the team.

Project Leadership Considerations

Uma acted responsibly as a project leader in overseeing the detailed plan development. She kept the customer's priorities in mind and worked in a logical order for the most part. Some project leaders would prefer to work through more of the WBS before finalizing the risk plan. Uma worked through the higher levels of the WBS with her core team, then had each core team member develop the details of their respective areas with their SMEs, and finally integrated the entire plan with anyone on the complete team making recommendations where there were conflicts. By using this method, Uma achieved efficiency in the work process and a more empowered workforce.

Once the WBS and risk plans were complete it was time to determine who should perform each identified task, what the durations and predecessors should be for each task, and how all this information should be combined into a workable schedule. Project leaders need to facilitate this activity, but do not have to perform it all personally. Technical leads, schedulers, and others should be able to perform much of this work. Nonetheless, project leaders need to understand what questions to ask, when to offer help, when to take over, and when to back off.

A final component of detailed project planning is the project budget. Top leadership in an organization sees a budget as a tool to assist in prioritizing organizational goals. Through the budget, top leaders allocate resources to selected projects, with more resources going to higher priority projects, and no (or few) resources going to low priority projects. Thus, as projects serve as means of accomplishing the goals of an organization, budgeting serves as the means of prioritizing those goals.

Project leaders can develop their detailed budget only if they have an understanding of the project WBS and schedule. Once these are understood, it is possible to determine the cost. If the expected cost is significantly different from the spending authority granted in the project charter, a serious discussion needs to take place. This could involve using a different approach, changing the project's scope or schedule, or canceling the project.

It was surprising and problematical that the detailed budget was shared with the whole team. While ideally teams share all information, it is debatable whether or not detailed budgets of other people's areas should be shared with the project team.

As project leaders oversee the development of the detailed project plans rather than get caught up in the details themselves, they need to:

- *Understand who gives good advice on the project plan and who gives poor advice.* Some project team members will have a much better understanding of how to plan than others.
- *Ensure that risks continue to be uncovered and addressed.* Hiding risks may be tempting to secure project approval, but gaining acceptance of a project with buried risks may be a Phyrric victory.
- *Encourage the project team to pursue innovative approaches where appropriate* and to reuse or adapt approaches developed previously as appropriate.
- *Understand that project team members both remember best and commit to those things that they "discover" on their own.* Orchestrate the plan development process so that team members can make "discoveries."
- *Realize that by active listening and following, a wise project leader both gains influence with her team and encourages the team to self-manage.*

Before this step was complete, it was very important that Uma ensure that everyone fully understood and was comfortable with the details of their own budget so that they could take "ownership" of their part of this project as well as the entire project.

Project Leadership Lesson: Planning—Project Details
A Project Leader Needs to:
Accept that the project team and SMEs will develop large parts of the project plan
Have the courage to challenge planning details
Exercise the wisdom to know when to trust and when to question.

INTEGRATE PROJECT PLANS

Uma then developed the integrated project plan to submit to the steering team and other stakeholders. The integrated project plan included the WBS, schedule, risk plan, and cost estimates. Uma wanted to create management plans for scope, time, and cost. Bob told Uma that they could work on these factors once the project was kicked off. He wanted to get the project started as there was pressure from Mark to get it going.

Project Leadership Considerations

Uma was facing a common project leadership dilemma. She was being pressured by powerful stakeholders to move forward, yet her core team members had stated they were not ready yet. This was a "leadership moment." She needed to recall the project priorities. In this case the non-negotiables were quality and time. Since she was within the allocated time, it became her responsibility to consider pushing back because moving too quickly could create an unacceptable risk.

While the key issue in developing integrated project plans is to ensure that the various components have consistency, sometimes there is time pressure to move along and iron out details later. This often creates problems that could have been easily handled with just a little more time in planning, but if discovered during execution, are much more disruptive to the project. The issue that faced the core team was whether they had enough information to complete the planning process. While very few teams feel they have all the information they would like, one component of project leadership is to know when the team has enough information to proceed.

Project leaders should remember a few key principles of project leadership planning at this time:

- *Understand a project at different levels*—as part of a larger system, as a system itself, and as a collection of parts. This understanding requires that the various parts of a project "fit" together in the integrated plan and reduces unpleasant surprises during project execution.

- *Remember that both numbers and ideas are important* in an integrated project plan. Many project participants primarily want to see or use either numbers or issues, but not both. An effective project leader needs to be comfortable with both.
- *Analyze complex tradeoffs* and understand their potential consequences. This can be helpful when making integration decisions.
- *Understand cause and effect relationships* so issues can be identified that, when improved, will also improve other areas. This also helps in making integration decisions.
- *Know when to make decisions and when to allow decision-making by the project team or by certain stakeholders.* Enlightened project leaders try to push the decision-making process to as low an organizational level as practical. This helps all project participants—the project team and other stakeholders—develop a sense of shared risk and reward. This ownership of decisions often is the extra intangible that helps project participants achieve a little more when faced with challenges during project execution.

Project Leadership Lesson: Planning—Project Integration

A Project Leader Needs to:

Accept that others can sometimes make better decisions than I can

Have the courage to make the decisions I should make

Exercise the wisdom to know which are which.

SELECT REMAINDER OF PROJECT PARTICIPANTS

Bob and Uma met with the core team members to discuss the remainder of the team. Uma had already sent an e-mail to the core team members asking them to consider people they would need for the rest of the project. Bob had identified the key project stakeholders who would need to play an active role if the project was to be successful. Based on the project plan, the team came up with subteams (listed in Table 3-4).

Sanjay said that he wanted to schedule the five consultants as soon as the project schedule was approved; he didn't want to lose good candidates because they were not scheduled soon enough. Uma wanted all the core team members to give her their subteam members' names and responsibilities. She wanted to prepare a responsibility matrix.

TABLE 3-4 B2B Project Subteam Responsibilities

Subteam and Leader	No. of Subteam Members	Responsibilities
Networking team—Scott	1 network administrator 1 systems administrator	Take care of network, security, firewall issues, systems, user management
Technical team—Sanjay	3 developers 2 contractors 3 consultants as needed at various stages	Programming and implementation
QA team—Paul	1 quality assurance engineer 2 testers at a later stage	Develop procedures for quality testing and prepare test plans
Business analysis team—Chris	4 business analysts	Work with different functional people to come up with requirements

Project Leadership Considerations

Project leaders should realize that selecting appropriate people for sub-teams has a great deal to do with project success. The comments on selecting key project participants made in Chapter 2 also apply here. However, at this level, technical competence may be more important. Many project managers and sponsors try to act in a collaborative manner with the members of the core project team and others in the organization as the remainder of the project participants are selected, but some do not. The subteam leader usually is in the best position to identify people who have the expertise needed. However, the sponsor or project manager may need to use their political acumen to actually get the person they want assigned to the project. Project leaders want to ensure that they are not simply "stuck" with workers that functional managers want to unload or with whoever happens to be available regardless of whether they are the best people for the job.

By totally delegating the responsibility of choosing subteam members to her core team, Uma abdicated responsibility. She could have empowered her core team by working collaboratively with them. The best long-term method of ensuring the ability to recruit eager and competent people is for a project leader to take care of both the projects and the people they are responsible for; such a project leader's reputation will spread. Wise project leaders want to be able to say convincingly, "If you work with me, you will be successful both on this project and after it. I can say that because that is what has happened to the people and the projects I have been associated with." In effect, the project leader is recruiting based upon both past success and future potential.

Everyone wants to work with a winner. If a project leader and a project both appear to be winners, willing and competent participants will be much easier to find.

One of the key aspects of the detailed project plan is assigning responsibility. If this is done clearly, it helps with identifying and recruiting the additional participants that are needed. The more specifically a project leader can delineate what a participant will be doing, when, under what conditions, etc., the easier it will be to find the right people for the project. Team needs and diversity of input also must be considered.

Project Leadership Lesson: Planning—Human Resources
A Project Leader Needs to:
Accept that we may not be able to have assigned to our project the particular subject matter experts we really want
Have the courage to understand the full range of the company's personnel needs
Exercise the wisdom to ensure that both project and other organizational needs are met.

DEVELOP COMMUNICATIONS PLAN

Uma decided to create the communications plan based on her prior experiences and then review it with the team. She decided that she would create a separate area in the company's intranet that would be accessible to the project team, steering committee, and stakeholders. The meeting minutes project folder would be available at every team meeting. Uma's communication plan is shown in Table 3-5.

TABLE 3-5 B2B Project Communications Plan

Communication	Who Creates	Frequency	Why
Project status report	Core team and SMEs	Weekly	To cover what was scheduled, what was completed, issues and their severity, dependencies affected by issues
Team project status reports	Team leads	Weekly	To summarize individual status reports and comments on the status
Project report	Project manager	Monthly	Financial details and project schedule status to sponsor, steering committee, and stakeholders
Team meetings	Project core team	Weekly initially; can be revised later	Jointly make decisions, uncover issues, monitor progress, and improve process
Project update	Project manager	Weekly	Keep sponsor up-to-date

Uma then invited all the team members to discuss the communication plan. Jeff asked Uma, "What about the meeting minutes? Do we copy everybody on the team?" Uma answered that subteam meeting minutes need to be sent to the core team members. The team leads could then decide if they need to copy the meeting minutes to any other stakeholders. The core team agreed to keep the communication channels open but not overloaded. Uma would also provide a weekly update to Bob. Steering team approval will be required at every milestone of the project. Uma and Bob shared the thought that it is their task to encourage the steering committee to periodically update the user community on the project's status and what to expect. Uma would be the primary communicator to Buslog.

Project Leadership Considerations

While much of what Uma did in developing the communications plan was appropriate, she missed a fundamental concept of good communication. The concept behind effective project communications is simple, even if the implementation is almost always a challenge. The concept is to first understand who needs to know what, in what format, at what time, under what circumstances. The rest of the concept is to construct a plan to give the various stakeholders the information they need in a timely fashion. Too much communication can be a problem, just as too little usually is. To understand what various stakeholders need to know, ask them! Uma did not ask anyone what they needed.

Project leaders should keep the following points in mind when developing a communications plan:

- Project leaders need to continually articulate their vision to all stakeholder groups.
- Project leaders should ensure that team members have regular, complete, and effective contact with their counterparts in the customer's organization. Engineers should talk with engineers, accountants with accountants, and programmers with programmers, etc. There may be a need to filter certain information, but that should not come at the expense of limiting important contacts.
- Project leaders need to develop well-grounded explanations for all questions that may arise. When possible, these should be developed before the need arises.
- The project communications plan should include clear guidelines for team meetings.

- The project communications plan should address the professional development of individuals as well as of the project team.
- The project communications plan should be an efficient means of organizing data and reporting results.
- Different people have different communication needs at different times. Keep asking if the current flow of information is adequate.

Project Leadership Lesson: Planning—Human Relations
A Project Leader Needs to:
Accept the fact that different project stakeholder have very diverse information desires
Have the courage to uncover and meet their true information needs
Exercise the wisdom to understand the difference between these desires and needs.

MOTIVATE ALL PARTICIPANTS

Bob realized the team had been working hard to develop the project plan and get the project rolling. He decided it was time to have some fun. He decided that they all would go out for dinner to a nice restaurant and then go out and play some pool. He asked his administrative assistant and Uma to plan some games and also invited the steering team to the dinner. Since Mark could not make it, he asked Gary to say a few words of appreciation to the team and emphasize what the project means to the company. Uma and Bob agreed that they will have some fun activities during every stage of the project (e.g., cookouts, different culture days, unannounced pizza parties). At every milestone the team members will be shown appreciation for the work done.

At dinner, Gary addressed the team by congratulating them on their success and said that he and every member of the steering team appreciated their contribution. He also made them feel that they had accomplished an important milestone and thanked them for that.

Project Leadership Considerations

Having a variety of "fun" activities is often a terrific idea; however, it is usually wise to let the group plan their own activities. Different people have very different ideas of "fun."

Throughout the project, project leaders have ongoing responsibilities to develop commitment in all stakeholders; the first part of this commitment is the unofficial desire or motivation on the part of everyone to do what is necessary. The second part is to publicly and officially commit. Motivating all participants is the unofficial commitment work that should take place during project planning in anticipation of everyone formally committing at the end of the planning stage.

Bob, Gary, and Uma focused their informal commitment efforts on the morale of the project team. While that is important, it is only one component. Each project leader should be articulating the benefits and excitement of the project and conveying the "what's in it for me" message. To motivate people it is wise to help them understand that the work they are doing is important, it is likely to be successful, and they will be rewarded fairly for their efforts. In this case Gary did articulate the vision for why the project is important. He could have told the team why he thought the current project approach would be successful.

We know the project team is celebrating, but what about all of the other project stakeholders? Have all the customer groups—internal and external—been involved in celebrating thus far? Do they share the project leaders' enthusiasm for the importance of the project?

Have all other stakeholders who could interfere with the project been communicated with? In some cases it may be difficult to excite them about the project. (Think of unwilling neighbors of a major construction project.) Have the project leaders at least dampened the negative feelings of those people who could be disruptive to the project if they were sufficiently antagonized?

If the project leaders have been communicating effectively and unofficially all along with all project stakeholders and key influencers, and if trust, integrity, and reciprocity have been established with them, then securing their formal approval should not be in doubt.

Project Leadership Lesson: Planning—Project Promotion
A Project Leader Needs to:
Accept the need to motivate all project participants
Have the courage to continually articulate the project vision and reasons it will succeed (especially to the reluctant participants)
Exercise the wisdom to understand how to motivate each participant.

SECURE STAKEHOLDER APPROVAL

Uma scheduled an internal project kickoff meeting, inviting all internal stakeholders, the steering team, the project core team, and all SMEs. The agenda for the meeting was to go through the detailed project plans, including the WBS, risks, schedule, and responsibilities with all stakeholders. Questions and answers would be a key part of this kick-off meeting.

A stakeholder from the accounting department was very upset with the partial implementation of the ERP system. Her assumption was that the accounting department may have to do dual data entry into both the legacy system and the new system for payments and invoices. She also said, "Every time IT says that they will automate something, then we have to learn a totally new system. By the time you get comfortable with it, it's time for them to implement something new again. When will they settle on one system?" Uma then explained, "This is a very strategic project for the company. The technical team will minimize the inconveniences by automating data transfer between the legacy system and the new system. The old legacy system has been customized heavily and documentation is not up to date; hence the users face problems if a new functionality is added. The new system is state-of-the art technology and it has the new functionalities we need, as our business has grown in the past couple of years. There will be user-friendly manuals to ease the implementation process." Bob confirmed that fact and pointed to the project activities that address those issues.

At the end of the internal project kick-off meeting, all internal stakeholders (including the steering team) approved the project plan. Then Bob, Uma, and the core team met with their customer counterparts in an external project kick-off meeting.

At the end of this meeting the team had also secured approval from Buslog, the external customer.

Project Leadership Considerations

Project planning often culminates in a formal project kick-off meeting with the intent of answering all questions and securing approval from all stakeholders to proceed. If all the other project leaders' planning tasks have been carried out well, the chances of securing approval are quite high. It is not uncommon for the project core team to first meet with all internal stakeholders to ensure that each of them fully understands and commits to the project plan. Then it is time to meet with the customer for concurrence.

In an ideal world the concerns of various stakeholders have been considered and there are no "surprises" at the kick-off meeting. In Uma's interaction with the accounting representative, she needed to be careful not to promise more than the project can deliver.

Project leaders should demonstrate that they understand the details in each area, but that they are concerned primarily with the overall project instead of any one portion. The project leaders often must convince reluctant stakeholders that their particular area may not get exactly what they prefer, but the project as a whole will be well served. Good communications planning and effective work on motivating these reluctant stakeholders in advance should help avoid disruption at the kick-off meeting.

Project Leadership Lesson: Planning—Commitment

A Project Leader Needs to:

Accept the fact that many diverse stakeholders must approve the project plan

Have the courage to secure acceptance by each

Exercise the wisdom to promise only what the team can deliver.

Once everyone has publicly and personally committed to the detailed project plan, the team is ready to begin project execution! Actually, on many projects, tasks and resources that require long lead times were probably preapproved in anticipation of the project plan being accepted. Time is an important factor to project leaders and they cannot afford to squander it.

CHAPTER 4

Project Executing

Project executing is the third of the four stages in the project lifecycle, as highlighted in Table 4-1. This is the time when most of the actual hands-on project work is accomplished and most of the money is spent as plans are implemented. In many types of projects, this stage is divided into more detailed stages. For example, on many information systems projects the executing stage may include development, coding, test, and deployment. Construction projects may include procurement, construction, and start-up as parts of project execution.

TABLE 4-1 Project Leader Responsibilities: Executing

Category of Project Leadership Task	Project Leadership Stage			
	Initiating	**Planning**	**Executing**	**Closing**
Project Priorities	Align project with parent organization	Understand and respond to the customer	Authorize work	Audit project
Project Details	Perform risk analysis	Oversee detailed plan development	Monitor progress and control changes	Terminate project
Project Integration	Justify and select project	Integrate project plans	Coordinate work across multiple projects	Capture and share lessons learned
Human Resources	Select key project participants	Select remainder of project participants	Supervise work performance	Reassign workers
Human Relations	Determine team operating methods	Develop communications plan	Lead teams	Reward and recognize participants
Project Promotion	Develop top management support	Motivate all participants	Maintain morale	Celebrate project completion
Project Commitment	Commit to project	Secure key stakeholder approval	Secure customer acceptance	Oversee administrative closure

Regardless of the substages that may be included in a particular type of project, all projects share certain types of project leadership tasks during project execution. These include:

- Authorize work
- Monitor progress and control changes
- Coordinate work across multiple projects
- Supervise work performance
- Lead teams
- Maintain morale
- Secure customer acceptance.

AUTHORIZE WORK

Sanjay, as a technical lead, wanted to schedule a couple of resources for training and he also wanted to hire one additional person from a consulting company. He felt he should talk this over with Uma, but Uma wasn't available. He decided to start negotiating with the consulting company for a good person for the best price. He also signed up two of his developers for specialized training at a cost of $6,000. He asked them to make reservations for training, airlines, and hotels using their corporate cards. He reviewed the contract with the legal department to make sure the contracts met legal requirements. He signed the contract with the consulting company for a consultant. Then Sanjay wondered if he was authorized to sign contracts. He decided to wait until he could meet with Uma.

The next day Sanjay met with Uma about these issues. Uma said she would have liked Sanjay to check with her before he authorized training. Sanjay responded by asking Uma to clarify what they, as team leads, can authorize and what they cannot.

Uma sent a memo to her core team reiterating that she directs and controls all work performed. She has control over high-level task assignment to the team leads and she controls and assigns the budget and master schedule. Each individual team lead can authorize expenditures below $2,500, but they must update her immediately. The team leads can authorize subtask assignments within their team. Any change in the schedule must be approved by Uma. All decisions also need prior approval.

Project Leadership Considerations

This B2B project example raises the first central issue regarding work authorization. Project leaders need to make clear who can authorize work, under what circumstances, and with what spending authority. The project leadership responsibilities described in the initiation and planning stages should have covered this issue. The detailed project plan, communications plan, and stakeholder approvals should all be used as guides in determining who can authorize project work. Sanjay was uncertain about the limits of his spending authority. Uma needed to decide this, but instead her memo appears to be an overreaction.

The second key issue in work authorization is the actual authorization itself. Regardless of the level of work or level of the project leader, he or she needs to be capable of making appropriate decisions on a timely basis. Decisions need to be made about which resources to use; when, where, and how to carry out specific work assignments; and a myriad of other issues. Even with very good project plans, many prioritization issues are settled by appropriate authorization decisions. Decision-makers need to have access to adequate data to make informed decisions. They also must have the skill and confidence to make those decisions.

Junior leaders generally have more time and are closer to the action, so they are sometimes more available to make timely decisions. However, senior project leaders often have more perspective and can understand broader issues more fully. The key is to groom the junior leaders to be able to make more decisions as they prove themselves capable by making good decisions on small matters. These issues concerning decision-making also apply to the other project leadership responsibilities during project execution.

Uma is sending a very controlling message to her team. If the expense is in the budget, why is it necessary to receive a second approval? Leaders need to be consistent in their approach. Why delegate all kinds of authority but require extra controls when it comes to money? Is it a trust issue? Most lists of leadership requirements include "trust." If followers are not trusted, they often feel rejected. Uma has been leading in a very sharing manner, showing that she trusts the judgments of others. So then why does she need to be "updated immediately" if an expenditure below $2,500 is made? This is using "power over" rather than "power with." She is not empowering her team members and they may well resent it.

Project Leadership Lesson: Executing—Project Priorities

A Project Leader Needs to:

Accept that others may control some work authorization decisions

Have the courage to take responsibility for all work authorization

Exercise the wisdom to ensure that the process is clear to all.

MONITOR PROGRESS AND CONTROL CHANGES

Buslog project manager Cecil called Uma and suggested that they would like to get an available-to-promise document after they receive a purchase order acknowledgment from CSM. Uma told Cecil that it would be an addition to the scope of what had been agreed upon and she would have to discuss it with her project core team before committing to it. Cecil mentioned that he was under the impression that CSM was totally committed to working with Buslog on process automation. Uma reinforced to Cecil that they are committed to working with Buslog for successful process automation but that because this transaction had not been included in the project plan, she had to go back to the core team and get their consensus and the steering team's input before committing to it. She told Cecil that she would get back to him in a couple of days.

Uma asked Chris and others in the order processing department if an available-to-promise document was an existing process between the two companies. An order processing clerk mentioned that it was the usual process and she was surprised that it wasn't included in the agreement. Uma called a core team meeting to discuss whether this additional functionality should be included in the scope. Bob felt that it should be. Uma added this to the project plan and called Cecil to inform him.

As development was being completed and the system was being configured, a business analyst wanted to add a few more fields to the purchase order. The technical team was upset because they would have to go back and redo some of the work they had already completed. Uma wanted the team to meet and freeze the design work so that development work could continue without any interference.

As these small issues came up and conflicts arose, Uma realized that she lacked a change control plan. She created a change request document template and communicated to the team that all change requests should be given to her and she would discuss them with appropriate members before authorizing them. The change request document is shown in Figure 4-1.

Uma was very clear to her core team that she expected them to enter the time for each and every scheduled activity. That way, actual performance could be compared with planned performance with respect to both cost and schedule.

Project Leadership Considerations

Not having a plan to deal with changes was a significant error. Why the whole team would need to be involved in a suggested change is puzzling. A

FIGURE 4-1   Project Change Request Form

Part One – to be filled out by Submitter
Submitter: _____ Phone: _____ Email: _____
Date of Submission _____
Type of Change: Problem _____   Enhancement _____
Recommended Priority: Critical: _____ High _____ Medium _____ Low _____
Description of proposed change:

Reason for change:

Estimated schedule impact:
Estimated cost impact:

Part Two – to be filled out by Technical Leads

Technical Area	Estimated Impact	Recommend (yes or no)	Signed
A	_____	_____	_____
B	_____	_____	_____
. . .	_____	_____	_____
X	_____	_____	_____

Part Three – to be filled out by Project Manager
Approved? _____   Date: _____
Rejected? _____   Why? _____
Deferred? _____   What more info needed? _____
Assigned priority: Critical _____ High _____ Medium _____ Low _____
Responsibility assigned to: _____
Tracking number: _____
Date completed: _____

good leader involves people who have a stake in a decision. Uma was wise
to check with the order department. When she found out this was standard
operating procedure, she should have simply told Cecil and apologized for the
error. Again, leadership requires the ability to admit error.

Project leaders need to ensure that appropriate change management procedures are in place. The change order form developed in the example (Figure
4-1) is a good one. The most important issue regarding a change management system is that it be used. A mediocre system that is used consistently
is far superior to a well-conceived system that is not used consistently. A key
ongoing responsibility of project leaders is to ensure that everyone is using a
change control system all the time. This requires discipline and is probably

most effective when the project leaders demonstrate by their actions that they use the change control system all the time and expect everyone else to do so as well. A simple system that is quick and easy to use is more likely to be used consistently since it will be less troublesome when people are under time pressure.

Project leaders need to be aware when there is a problem so they can take appropriate corrective action in a timely manner. Many problems, if discovered quickly, are easy to rectify. Those same problems, if allowed to fester, can be much more expensive, time-consuming, and difficult to resolve. Thus, project leaders need to "reward" rather than "shoot" messengers of bad news. A wise project leader develops her project into a learning organization with an emphasis on identifying problems as quickly as possible, correcting them, and removing the underlying causes so they do not reappear. If a project leader has previously done a good job of overseeing the development of detailed project plans, integrating them, and developing appropriate communication systems, she should be rewarded with an early warning system for problems.

Project leaders need to keep in mind a number of additional issues as they monitor progress and control changes. For example:

- The project scope and deliverables should be in writing, spelled out in detail, in a form that everyone who reads will interpret in the same way. Wise project leaders understand on one hand the customer's sense of urgency in performing the project and on the other hand the change management problems that occur with starting poorly planned projects. They wrestle with this contradiction, trying to find an acceptable balance.
- "Touchpoints" are places in a project where work is passed from one person or group to another or where the work of one project intersects the work of another project or the ongoing work of the parent or customer's organization. Wise project managers challenge their project teams to identify touchpoints in advance that may cause them trouble (some of this should have been done during risk planning and communication planning), but much of it continues throughout project execution. These touchpoints should be carefully monitored and controlled.
- If the project leaders are effective in creating a learning organization, many opportunities for improvement should appear. Project leaders need to prioritize and continually reprioritize these opportunities.
- Project leaders need to set the example by personally using continuous improvement and insisting that others do so as well.

- Project leaders should set good examples by admitting mistakes, accepting blame, and changing systems so the same mistakes do not happen again.
- Effective project leaders see both problems and solutions before others do. This early insight requires knowing what to monitor, being frequently available for the monitoring (including many informal contacts with all sorts of project participants and other stakeholders), and having the judgment that comes from experience. Once project leaders see problems or solutions, they need to take action or create a situation whereby project participants can also discover the problems and solutions and take action on their own.
- Project leaders need to learn who gives good advice and who does not. They need to know whose opinion can be trusted. Project leaders should have strategies for helping those who do not yet have the judgment to give good advice.
- When controlling change (and when performing many other project leadership responsibilities), project leaders need to be effective negotiators. This is such an important skill that project leaders should consider taking some professional training in it.

Project Leadership Lesson: Executing—Project Details
A Project Leader Needs to:
Accept that many situations will cause changes to the project
Have the courage to insist on disciplined use of a change control system
Exercise the wisdom to make it simple.

COORDINATE WORK ACROSS MULTIPLE PROJECTS

During one of the project status meetings, Rob told Uma, "Since we have a new customer, I am being assigned to another project, which is to establish business processes with the new customer. So I can't be available for the technical people if they need any clarifications immediately." Uma asked Rob about his time on the other project, and Rob replied that it involved a couple of full-time weeks. Sanjay said that could be a problem for his team since they are in the process of performing some critical project activities. Uma asked if Chris' team could handle being a first level of support to Sanjay's team if Rob explained the process to them. Rob and Chris agreed to it.

The team complained that some of the stakeholders were not available to view the results of unit testing. Uma wanted the team to be able to inform stakeholders in advance when they might need them, since she understands that they each also have functional responsibilities.

Project Leadership Considerations

Most organizations will have multiple projects and many ongoing work activities occurring simultaneously. While some project team members will work primarily on one or a limited number of projects and have a limited number of ongoing responsibilities, others have many more varied responsibilities. Project leaders need to help everyone associated with the project balance the needs of trying to accomplish the project—sometimes in the face of severe difficulties—with the needs of other projects and other goals of the parent organization. This can be one of the more interesting paradoxes for project leaders since they are primarily responsible for accomplishing their projects, yet they need to be responsible members of their parent organization and keep the bigger picture in mind. Project leaders need to communicate both of these perspectives to the project team as often as needed.

To be successful at this balancing act, project leaders need to have the ability to:

- See the big picture and understand corporate strategic needs
- Analyze complex tradeoffs and understand their consequences, especially when multiple projects or multiple organizations are involved
- Understand their projects at multiple levels—as part of the larger organization, as a system itself, and as a collection of parts
- Make timely and sound decisions individually and facilitate groups such as project core teams and other stakeholders so they can also make timely and sound decisions
- Identify "touchpoints" in advance and continually monitor them
- Coordinate work, especially between their project and other work responsibilities, and understand how work assignments in one area impact other areas.

Project Leadership Lesson: Executing— Project Integration

A Project Leader Needs to:

Accept that other important work of the organization needs to take place

Have the courage to continually push for successful completion of this project

Exercise the wisdom to resolve conflicts between other work and this project.

SUPERVISE WORK PERFORMANCE

Uma closely monitored the quantitative performance of the project by comparing actual work completed to budgeted work that should be complete. She also spent time around the project core team to find out if they had any issues affecting their performance.

Scott stopped by Uma's office one day to discuss an issue regarding one of his team members. Tom, the systems administrator (who is a consultant from another company), had not been performing well during the last couple of weeks. He seemed to be preoccupied and had made a couple of mistakes. Since these were in the development and testing environment, the consequences were controllable. Scott mentioned that Tom is a very intelligent person and it is not his usual habit to make these types of mistakes. He wanted Uma's advice on how to deal with the situation. Uma advised Scott to take Tom out for lunch, talk to him casually, and find out if he is having any personal problems.

Over lunch, when Scott asked him if there were any problems, Tom mentioned to him that his company had announced a merger with another solutions company; there would be a reduction in force and he was worried about it. Scott assured Tom that he would do anything he could to help him be secure in his job. Scott returned from lunch and updated Uma. Uma talked this issue over with Gary, who told her that Tom had been a consultant with the company for the last six years and was a valuable asset. If Tom were laid off, Gary could secure an agreement from Tom's company to allow him to work as independent consultant for the duration of the project. Gary told Uma that, if Tom is interested, he could perhaps join CSM later. Uma asked Scott to convey this message to Tom. Tom felt secure and his performance improved.

Jeff and Elizabeth developed a personal relationship during the course of the project, but recently their relationship ended. As this became public, some of the team members avoided having Elizabeth and Jeff in the same meeting. As the project was nearing the completion stage, Elizabeth's team had a major role in accepting the system for day-to-day operations. Uma talked with Jeff and Elizabeth separately to ensure that their personal issues didn't impact the team's performance.

Project Leadership Considerations

Scott could have simply stated to Tom in a private setting, "I noticed that you made two errors recently. This is so unlike you. Is anything getting in your way? Is there any way I can be helpful?" A skilled leader speaks to the behavior and the facts, not to assumptions.

In the second situation, private meetings may or may not be wise. Again, a simple factual statement to the team is usually best. The leader might say to the team, "I am aware that some team members are not being invited to meetings they should attend. That can negatively impact the project. I assume that everyone will behave responsibly and not let any external matters affect how we treat each other."

In supervising work performance, project leaders need to define their work expectations to enable the individual contributors to understand what they are supposed to do, how they should do it, and their degree of freedom. Then the project leaders need to assess the work as it is being performed so they can apprise the workers how their actual performance compares with the expectations. The twin goals at this point are to (1) close the gap between the performance and the expectation so the project work can be completed as planned, and (2) help the workers improve.

A key balancing act at this point is to determine how much focus should be on achieving the project goals versus how much time should be spent on improving individual work performance. In most situations the work of the project cannot be sacrificed for improved worker training and education. A wise project leader will learn how to keep the focus squarely on project work performance while simultaneously giving individual workers immediate feedback that will help in their growth and development.

A few ideas project leaders may want to keep in mind as they supervise work performance include:

- Lead by example so you can establish trust, integrity, and mutual sharing in both work performance and professional growth and development. A wise leader will seize opportunities to help the hands-on workers improve and to help himself improve.
- Involve workers in communicating work progress. Project leaders are almost always challenged in terms of time. If she needs to monitor every worker's performance closely, a project leader may be very limited in her ability to complete a myriad of other project leadership responsibilities. Along with laying out expectations for the work, she also should lay out expectations for reporting the work. (This should have been accomplished in communications planning.) Wise project leaders will begin to understand which workers can be trusted to report their work progress at less frequent intervals versus those who need to be managed more closely.

- Regard helping others reach their potential as a key responsibility and a source of personal fulfillment. A project leader should help individuals assess their strengths and weaknesses as a means of facilitating their professional growth.
- Be a good trainer and mentor. Some feedback discovered while supervising work performance will suggest group training needs and some will suggest individual mentoring as the preferred vehicle for improvement. The old saying that "when the pupil is ready the teacher will appear" pertains here. The project leader needs to help the individual workers understand when a teacher is needed and often must be that teacher herself. Project leaders need to decide when more efficient group training is sufficient versus when more time-consuming mentoring is needed.

Project Leadership Lesson: Executing—Human Resources

A Project Leader Needs to:

Accept that actual project results need to be compared to planned project results

Have the courage to uncover reasons for work performance problems

Exercise the wisdom to do so in a fair yet effective manner.

LEAD TEAMS

The development team was ready to work on the business-to-business process. This was the time for joint efforts between CSM and Buslog. A virtual combined project team is formed. The CSM project team consisted of Uma, Sanjay, Chris, and two developers. The Buslog project team included Cecil, the project manager, Bev Oswald, and three developers.

Buslog's developers were in Germany and its business analysts were in Florida. The time zones varied considerably, and it became a nightmare for communications. Uma took the lead in developing a communications plan to make this virtual team work. Since this was a short-term project, at the end of every working day each member sent a status report to all the members of the team. Every week a videoconference took place. E-mail was the primary mode of communication. This process was viewed as a project within a project since it had a separate project plan and schedule. Uma led both teams. Since the main project was in the executing phase, Uma had more free time and she could provide more involvement in this combined project.

Project Leadership Considerations

Uma saw a problem, and, based on her experience, she developed a solution. She asked the team to try this process and they all saw its value. During the implementing stage she needed to be seen as a helpful, creative, and effective resource. It appears she successfully played these roles in this situation.

Leading teams involves three major areas in which effective project leaders need to display knowledge, skills, and commitments. They need to (1) understand how project teams develop and evolve, (2) facilitate project team progress, and (3) role-model effective behavior.

Classic team development literature describes forming, storming, norming, and performing as the four developmental stages teams can be expected to go through.[1] Project teams also experience a fifth stage: adjourning, at which time the teams complete their project work. (Chapter 5 covers the adjourning, or closing, stage.)

In executing the work of a project, all participants—senior project leaders, junior project leaders, hands-on project workers, and other stakeholders—can be considered part of the project team. Most team suggestions are directed toward small teams of hands-on workers who are often working together full-time. In many project situations, however, some of the essential participants are working only very part-time on a project. Additionally, some have heavier work involvement at different stages of the project's lifecycle. For example, senior project leadership will likely have a much heavier load very early in the project, junior project leadership's heavy load will start during planning, and hands-on workers' heavy load will be during project executing. The teamwork implication arising from this work pattern is that often those whose work involvement started much earlier are at a more advanced stage in the team development cycle than those who are newer to the project. Project leaders need to be able to deal with this disparity.

To be effective, project leaders need to understand the dynamics of each stage of team development. As teams are forming, project leaders will help team members develop commitment and trust with their teammates, leaders, and other project stakeholders. As teams enter into storming, it is often because of diversity in values, experiences, beliefs, personality, etc., on the part of some of the project team.

Project leaders need to act as facilitators. There are times when a project leader must impose her will to get things done in a hurry, but as often as possible, leading should be performed in a facilitating style. As she tries to lead in a facilitating style, a project leader should keep in mind:

- *Share leadership when possible.* It helps team members develop, gives each more of a sense of project ownership, and often allows much more rapid completion of project work.
- *Assess project team strengths and weaknesses* to facilitate growth. The Project Leadership Assessment: Team in Appendix C can be used for this assessment.
- In addition to helping individuals reach their potential, *help teams reach their collective potential.* If a project leader is effective in this regard, the team will move quickly through the early stages of team development and spend more of their time as a highly effective performing team. Also, when setbacks occur, the project team will retrace its steps through team development more quickly.
- *Encourage team self-management* by continuing to have the project team use the operating methods and communications plan they developed during project planning and the charter they developed during project initiating. If they use these documents, the team should not have to appeal to their leaders too often for guidance.
- *Remove obstacles* that are beyond the authority of the teams to remove themselves. In this sense, project leaders help manage the boundaries between the project team and all others.

A third major component of leading project teams is for leaders to serve as role models. If teams are to be effective, individual members of the teams need to behave in certain ways that can be enhanced by the team leaders' example. Some of these include:

- *Strive for interpersonal effectiveness* first in oneself and then in others. People are much more likely to exert the extra effort required to excel if they see their leaders doing so.
- *Strive to establish trust, integrity, and reciprocity* with everyone. This often requires extra effort, but is well worth it.
- *Seek help when needed.* We all need help in performing our work on occasion, but some project leaders may feel it is a sign of weakness to ask for help. On the contrary, not asking for help when necessary is a sign of immaturity that will not only diminish one's personal performance but will jeopardize the entire project. All project participants need to develop an understanding of when to ask for help and when to just get the job done themselves.

Project Leadership Lesson: Executing—Human Relations
A Project Leader Needs to:
Accept the need for sometimes large, diverse, changing, or virtual project teams
Have the courage to lead in a facilitating manner guided by the project charter, operating methods, and communications plan
Exercise the wisdom to understand when to intervene and when to let the team struggle.

MAINTAIN MORALE

Integration testing was in full progress using the integration test plans. Stakeholders were heavily involved in testing. One of the stakeholders in the order processing department was very unhappy about the way special orders were being handled in the system. He complained to everyone he saw that the new system was worse than the old system, and the QA team and business analysts were getting annoyed by his complaints. The connectivity testing between CSM and Buslog was not going as planned. On the CSM side, since they had a networking person on the team, it was convenient to deal with network issues between the two companies. But, on the Buslog side, the networking people were in a different location and there were communications issues. The developers were getting impatient. Many members of the team were showing the stress of attempting to complete the project on time.

Uma and Bob were wondering what to do to boost the morale of the team and improve the process. They decided to have a day to celebrate all the completed milestones of the project and make the team members feel good. They also had to figure out how to solve the problems and reduce tensions. They decided to meet with the stakeholders and team members separately to identify issues and solutions. They also decided to talk to the project manager and sponsor at Buslog to identify their issues in connectivity testing.

Project Leadership Considerations

Project leaders must work to keep the project team, client, suppliers, executive management, and themselves motivated. Uma and Bob were appropriate as far as they went by noticing problems and creating ways to celebrate milestone completion. Some organizations do not take time to celebrate the completion of important milestones. Properly executed, these celebrations can really help lift the team's morale. Bob and Uma also tried to identify issues and develop solutions in a participative manner with their team.

Celebrations do not solve all problems, however. The issue here is a real one; each team has different resources and different needs. Uma and Bob need to suggest creative ways of solving the actual problems. Once they are solved and appropriate milestones are met, a celebration of the group's choosing may well be appropriate.

Project leaders should keep a number of broad considerations in mind as they attempt to keep up project team morale:

- Project leaders need to spend time meeting people and communicating their vision for the project. They also need to hear and reinforce the visions each stakeholder brings to the project. This can be an effective, proactive way of maintaining morale.
- Project leaders should use empowerment (as Uma and Bob usually do) instead of fear. In the heat of the moment, when people are trying to meet critical deadlines, it is sometimes tempting for a project leader to order, threaten, or coerce actions. While this may feel like it is solving a near-term problem, it often makes morale more difficult to maintain.
- Project leaders who have a track record of success or can give their teams other reasons to believe that all will be okay have something tangible to offer. People need to have specific solutions to keep up their morale.
- Project leaders often do not immediately understand all that their team members are trying to tell them. It sometimes behooves a project leader to become a better listener, often a follower, until they do understand. This can be very motivating for the team member who takes the lead in the situation.
- Project leaders need to understand that conflict is often the cause of poor morale. The ability to identify and resolve conflict is critical for project leaders. Wise project leaders understand that some conflict—that is, conflict that can energize people with alternative approaches to consider—can be beneficial. However, conflict that becomes too intense and personal can be detrimental to project success.
- Project leaders need to be able to diagnose and manage stress both in themselves and in others. Projects can be highly charged activities with tight timelines, severe constraints, and high expectations. While some people thrive in this environment, others find it very stressful. Project leaders need to develop methods of relieving their own stress (e.g., yoga, poker, running) and to encourage team members to do the same.

Project Leadership Lesson: Executing—Project Promotion
A Project Leader Needs to:
Accept that projects can be hard work with stressful periods
Have the courage to confront problems and celebrate success
Exercise the wisdom to understand when each is important and appropriate.

SECURE CUSTOMER ACCEPTANCE

The QA teams performed a full integration test involving transactions between Buslog and CSM. All the stakeholders were involved in checking the results of the test, which turned out to be satisfactory. Both CSM and Buslog monitored the performance of the transaction, went through all business case scenarios, and verified the results. The results were satisfactory and were accepted by the order processing and ASN departments. Most importantly, the external customer, Buslog, was also satisfied.

The next step in the project plan was to do a stress testing involving 1,000 purchase orders a day. The stress testing was conducted for a week, with the speed and performance of the business process carefully monitored. During the process of stress testing, performance was an issue since it took half an hour to process 100 purchase orders. This was not acceptable to CSM. The business-to-business people were saying that the reason for such slow performance was either the network or the new order processing system. They needed a person who knew the ERP system as well as networking, systems administration, and business-to-business software to solve the problem. A special consultant was brought in to tune the system. The testers then signed off on the QA test plan.

The team worked on a transition* document to explain the roles and responsibilities for maintenance of the system. End user training was scheduled for over a week to educate all employees involved with the new system. Buslog was satisfied with the test results. The system went through a phase of parallel testing, and then the operations team took over maintenance of the system. All documentation was handed over to the operations and IT teams.

The system went into production on schedule, and the project team celebrated the event by going out for dinner.

Project Leadership Considerations

The project leaders used extensive testing to convince the customer that the project results were acceptable. Many kinds of projects involve demonstration or testing of some sort. Of course, the project leaders must ensure that the project deliverables will satisfy all of the testing and validation requirements. However, project leaders should develop a couple of other skills if they are to secure customer approval.

First, project leaders need to be able to understand the customer's culture. The better project leaders understand the customer's culture, the better they can lead the actual project development and the better they can convince the customer that things are fine. In other words, the actual deliverables of the project can be made more useful to the customer, and the customer's perception can be influenced. These activities, guided by an understanding of the customer, should culminate in customer acceptance of the project deliverables.

Second, project leaders frequently need to negotiate. This skill can be useful in many circumstances, such as agreeing on the charter terms and securing resources for project work. Project leaders might need to negotiate tradeoffs between some aspect of the project that is not fully developed versus another area in which the client can get more than he bargained for.

The B2B project team successfully addressed the technical part of securing customer acceptance by passing rigorous performance tests. They also created a transition document to help the customer use the system effectively, thereby successfully addressing the need for customer understanding.

Project Leadership Lesson: Executing—Commitment

A Project Leader Needs to:

Accept that understanding the customer is important in securing customer acceptance

Have the courage to rigorously prove that the project deliverables work correctly

Exercise the wisdom to negotiate tradeoffs to satisfy the client.

Now that the customer has accepted the project deliverables, it is time to proceed to project closing.

NOTE

1. Peter R. Scholtes *et al.*, *The Team Handbook*, 2nd ed. (Madison, WI: Joiner Associates, 1996).

CHAPTER 5

Project Closing

losing is the final stage of the project leadership responsibilities model, as highlighted in Table 5-1. Closing is a fundamental element of the management of any project. By its very definition, a project is a temporary endeavor so there must be an ending. Despite the obvious importance of project closing, the specifics are often not performed well and sometimes not performed at all.

TABLE 5-1 Project Leader Responsibilities: Closing

Category of Project Leadership Task	Project Leadership Stage			
	Initiating	Planning	Executing	Closing
Project Priorities	Align project with parent organization	Understand and respond to the customer	Authorize work	Audit project
Project Details	Perform risk analysis	Oversee detailed plan development	Monitor progress and control changes	Terminate project
Project Integration	Justify and select project	Integrate project plans	Coordinate work across multiple projects	Capture and share lessons learned
Human Resources	Select key project participants	Select remainder of project participants	Supervise work performance	Reassign workers
Human Relations	Determine team operating methods	Develop communications plan	Lead teams	Reward and recognize participants
Project Promotion	Develop top management support	Motivate all participants	Maintain morale	Celebrate project completion
Project Commitment	Commit to project	Secure key stakeholder approval	Secure customer acceptance	Oversee administrative closure

As in the previous stages in the project lifecycle, seven project leadership tasks are involved in this stage:

- Audit project
- Terminate project
- Capture and share lessons learned
- Reassign workers
- Reward and recognize participants
- Celebrate project completion
- Oversee administrative closure.

AUDIT PROJECT

At CSM, the project office had an audit team that reviewed all projects. The audit team evaluated the financial schedule and the quality of the project results. The audit team found that the project was a week behind schedule. The audit report noted that for IT projects dealing with online transactions, stress testing is very important. The audit team suggested that the reasons for the success of this project were senior management support and the consistency of project priorities. It was also found that not all consultants hired were highly successful and that some of them had to be changed in the course of the project.

Project Leadership Considerations

The B2B audit report summary included reasons for the schedule slippage as well as reasons for the overall project success. While there is not enough detail to comment on the completeness of the project audit, at least it was performed and it addressed several areas.

The purposes for conducting project audits are to determine: how well the project priorities (scope, quality, schedule, and cost) were achieved; the reasons for the success (or lack of success) in achieving each priority; and any corrective actions that are needed.

The project audit serves a very useful function if it is performed in a positive manner. That is, it should be used to look for solutions, not to place blame. Project audits provide a thorough and methodical review of all aspects of a project and can be implemented in various ways. Some companies have a quality assurance group that performs the project audit, some have project audit teams as a function of the project office, and yet others have an auditing function in their accounting group.

Project audits are a useful tool for gathering the information needed to ensure that all deliverables are complete, quality is acceptable, and all open contractual issues are resolved. Project audits are normally performed at the end of the project, but can occur at any time during the project lifecycle. Project audits that occur earlier in a project can provide a measuring stick to see how a project is doing and, if necessary, make recommendations for corrective actions. Project audits performed during closing do not help the current project, but they capture lessons learned for future projects and also serve as a performance measure for the project manager and the project team.

Informal methods of conducting project audits include:

- Mutual nonthreatening review of each other's project by two project managers
- Requesting a review of your project by an independent consultant or the project office staff
- Internal team review to walk through the project and determine how it is progressing.

The project audit activities cover all aspects of project leadership. The project leader needs to take an active role in the analysis of the results of the audit and, if changes are required, take a positive approach to communicating and effecting the changes. The core team members need to look at the project audit in a positive light and assist in making any needed corrective actions now or on future projects. The organization needs to support this effort and assist by providing adequate resources to successfully complete the project audit and take any necessary corrective actions.

Project Leadership Lesson: Closing—Project Priorities

A Project Leader Needs to:

Accept that all projects can be improved through timely and thoughtful audits
Have the courage to learn from project audits
Exercise the wisdom to look for solutions instead of culprits.

TERMINATE PROJECT

Rob was working on a project to put business processes in place for a customer, SOTA. After a couple of months of work, SOTA was acquired by North Central Corp. and there were strains in the business relationship with the new owners. CSM's executive team decided to stop all internal projects dealing with North Central Corp. until they improved the business relationship. The executive team felt it was not wise to spend money on projects unless the customer relationship was solid.

Project Leadership Considerations

CSM's executive team appears to have made a sensible decision in stopping internal projects involving their customer, North Central Corp. They have learned that without positive business relationships, joint business ventures often fail. However, nothing is said about their plan to build this relationship. A corollary challenge to the executive team is to look internally for systematic issues that led to this situation.

One responsibility of project leaders is to be a strong advocate for their project, especially in difficult times. A contrasting responsibility, however, is to recommend project termination when it is appropriate.

Terminating a project is a very difficult task. Responsible project termination decisions require a detailed understanding of performance as well as an understanding of the personal and organizational impact of a termination. In some organizational cultures, terminating a project is tantamount to terminating the careers of the individuals involved. Frequently, projects need to be terminated for reasons that have nothing to do with the project leader or the project team, such as:

- Changes in technology have rendered the product obsolete
- The business need that caused the project charter to be written is no longer valid
- Technological difficulties make the approach to the problem difficult or impossible or the cost is too high
- The market has changed and the product is no longer needed or economically feasible.

One essential project leadership skill is to have the courage and foresight to terminate projects when necessary. For example, many research and development organizations expect to terminate many projects before one is commercially successful. These organizations often encourage early project termination since the later a project is terminated, the more money, personnel, and other resources are wasted. It is also not uncommon that the thought of terminating a project is much worse than the results of actually doing it. Although this seems to be a task-oriented issue, it affects all aspects of project leadership. Virtually all the stakeholders need to be informed and involved in the decision. The responsibility to recommend that a project be terminated rests with any one of the stakeholders that feel it is justified. The project leader should not have to bear the full responsibility of making the recommendation.

In Western culture, people often think in terms of completion with winners and losers. Terminating a project in this context appears to be losing. In fact, leaders who, by virtue of their termination recommendation, display the ethical wisdom of minimizing organizational waste and the value of honest and open communication should be rewarded. They are taking the long-term view of doing what is best for everyone.

Project Leadership Lesson: Closing—Project Details
A Project Leader Needs to:
Accept that some projects should not be completed
Have the courage to make a decision in the best interest of the organization
Exercise the wisdom to know whether to continue or to terminate the project.

CAPTURE AND SHARE LESSONS LEARNED

After the audit was performed, Gary asked Uma how lessons learned were captured. Because CSM hoped to have more B2B projects, these lessons would be helpful. The team went through the entire project structure and captured lessons learned from each stage. The team also captured the stakeholders' reaction.

Project Leadership Considerations

One method of integration is to capture and use project lessons learned. These enable project teams to perform better in subsequent project stages and on future projects.

Most organizations do not handle lessons learned very well. Sometimes the information is never gathered. Sometimes the information is gathered, but very few, if any, have access to it. Frequently, the information is gathered, organized, and available, but no one looks at it. Organizations will unfortunately tend to make the same mistakes repeatedly because they do not learn from their prior mistakes.

Another issue with lessons learned is the timing of when they are captured. If a project leader and the team decide to wait until the end of the project to gather all the lessons learned information, a number of things can impede the process or the quality of the results, such as:
- Team members with knowledge of the events may have departed to work on other projects
- On long projects, the project team members may have forgotten key points that occurred early in the project lifecycle
- At the end of the project, there may be insufficient time or budget left to capture lessons learned effectively.

The project leader needs to include capturing lessons learned as a task in the project plan with resources assigned. Lessons-learned tasks, including gathering, compiling, analyzing, and disseminating information, should take place at the end of each project lifecycle stage.

Project leadership considerations related to the capturing and sharing of lessons learned include:

- Project leaders should develop learning organizations
- Project leaders should set the example of using continuous improvement
- Project leaders should actively listen
- Project organizations should develop and use a methodology to consistently gather, share, and benefit from the lessons learned
- Project leaders should incorporate previous learning so that the project can be "jump started"
- Project leaders should discover innovative ideas that can be pursued to improve the processes.

Project Leadership Lesson: Closing—Project Integration

A Project Leader Needs to:

Accept that it is often difficult to capture project lessons

Have the courage to insist that lessons learned are captured

Exercise the wisdom to actually use the lessons learned on future projects.

REASSIGN WORKERS

Uma and Bob worked with the functional managers to reassign team members back to their respective functional departments. Some consultants would continue maintaining the system for a period of time and others would be leaving CSM. By identifying the new projects or roles for the team members even before the project went into production, Uma and Bob were able to decrease the stress that project closure often causes for team members. Bob arranged for Uma to manage a larger project that he would sponsor.

Project Leadership Considerations

Reassignment of personnel is the responsibility of the project leader. The project leader must care for and see that the team members are reassigned in a manner that is helpful to each team member's career and professional development. In a large organization, the project leader may need to work with many people such as the human resources department, the project management office, other project leaders, and functional managers in an effort to make the best fit possible. The team members are assets of the company and the project leader has a responsibility to develop and protect them.

The reassignment of the project team to a new project or other assignments should be considered renewing as opposed to ending. It may be necessary to place some team members outside of the company or even with a competitor. It is the project leader's responsibility to see that the team members are taken care of and to find appropriate new assignments for them.

Project Leadership Lesson: Closing— Human Resources
A Project Leader Needs to:
Accept that project participants will move on to other work
Have the courage to help them secure appropriate assignments
Exercise the wisdom to balance making a positive impact on their careers with project needs.

REWARD AND RECOGNIZE PARTICIPANTS

This project was considered successful since Buslog was very happy with the results. Bob convinced senior management to permit the team to have a big dinner party to celebrate the success. All project participants, including consultants and senior representatives, were invited. Mark (CSM's CEO) congratulated everyone on the team for their success and asked for their continued support in future projects. Bob congratulated Uma and her team for making this project a success. He also announced that the bonus would be paid in the next month. Uma had gifts for team members who went beyond the call of duty for implementation. The event was a mixture of joy and sadness as team was being dispersed.

Project Leadership Considerations

B2B project leaders did a good job recognizing and rewarding their participants. Recognition included the dinner, with each participant congratulated by Mark. Rewards included both across-the-board bonuses for everyone and individual gifts for superior performers. While there are many advantages and disadvantages of both across-the-board and targeted incentives, the B2B project leaders attempted to reach a balance. Project leaders define, develop, review, and reward performance.

Recognizing and rewarding accomplishments is a very important, but sometimes neglected, aspect of project leadership. It is appropriate to thank the team members when they do well. This informal approach to recognition is important, but it is not enough. Formal recognition is very important and can include the following:

- Recognition in the company newsletter
- Recognition in a company news release
- Recognition through a picture or article in the business section of the hometown newspaper
- Recognition at professional association meetings or in industry trade journals or magazines
- Recognition at a special end-of-project celebration
- Recognition at a company function, such as an awards dinner, company picnic, or holiday party.

There are no doubt other creative ways to recognize teams and team members for their contributions and achievements. As mentioned, providing higher levels of empowerment for the team or team members, such as a higher level approval authority or setting of the project team work timeframes, could be a way to recognize achievements. Basically it can be anything that the project team members and others will perceive as being of value to them.

Rewards do not have to financial, but cash bonuses are always a nice way to reward high achievement. People seem to work harder when they feel their compensation is tied to their performance. Some other ways to reward team members might include:

- A promotion or pay raise out of the normal cycle to reward superior initiative or performance
- Use of a company vehicle for some period of time
- Use of a special reserved parking space for some period of time
- Tickets to a sporting or entertainment event
- Use of a company recreational facility
- An expense-paid trip to a nice vacation spot
- An expense-paid weekend away for two at a nice hotel or resort.

The thing to remember is that recognition and rewards are another form of investment in your most valuable asset as a project leader: your people.

Project Leadership Lesson: Closing—Human Relations
A Project Leader Needs to:
Accept that project participants' contributions may vary considerably
Have the courage to recognize the good and reprimand the bad contributions
Exercise the wisdom to know when to reward and when to reprimand.

CELEBRATE PROJECT COMPLETION

CSM combined the dinner to celebrate project completion with the individual recognition of project participants.

Project Leadership Considerations

End-of-project celebrations can serve several functions. They can relieve the stress participants may have felt in a highly charged project. Celebrations are also a wonderful opportunity for project leaders to remind the participants how important their work really was. Most people are energized by performing worthwhile work.[1] Participants thus energized will be eager to work with the same project leaders and teams on future projects.

A celebration is the perfect forum for the project leader to reward and recognize participants. Make it an important event that is fun and something that people will remember and want to do again.

CSM's decision to combine participant reward and recognition with the ending celebration makes sense. However, they missed an opportunity to energize their project participants by reminding them of the importance of their results.

Project Leadership Lesson: Closing—Project Promotion
A Project Leader Needs to:
Accept that both teams and individuals need celebration
Have the courage to promote future project teamwork
Exercise the wisdom to know when to celebrate project accomplishments and when to look toward the future.

OVERSEE ADMINISTRATIVE CLOSURE

The project team was dispersed. The order processing system was turned over to the operations department. Uma met with the accounting department and handed over all the financial documents of the project so that accounting could close the books on the project.

Project Leadership Considerations

Uma correctly had someone from accounting close the books; however, she is still responsible for ensuring that this is done correctly and should verify the work. Uma should also have ensured that other items were completed as part of project administrative closure.

One of the final responsibilities requiring project leaders' commitment is to oversee project administrative closure. This is largely a communications function, but also involves some specific tasks that need to be accomplished, such as ensuring that:

- All the work packages in the WBS structure are completed
- All the account codes for the project in the accounting system are closed so people can no longer charge to the project's accounts
- All final reports are prepared and distributed
- All vendors, suppliers, and subcontractors are paid
- All final invoicing is performed and payments are received.

Project Leadership Lesson: Closing—Commitment
A Project Leader Needs to:
Accept that there are many administrative details that must be accomplished at project closing
Have the courage to insist that these details get completed
Exercise the wisdom to know when to move on.

NOTE

1. Ken Blanchard and Sheldon Bowles, *Gung Ho: Turn On the People in Any Organization* (New York: William Morrow and Company, Inc., 1998).

CHAPTER 6

Project Leadership Challenges

People have always planned, organized, implemented, and evaluated projects of many sizes and varieties. Until the industrial revolution, this was done in a very informal manner.

By the late nineteenth century, an ever-increasing amount of work was being mechanized and the study of mass production management was born. Many of the planning, organizing, leading, and controlling concepts and techniques that were developed at this time are still in use and also form a foundation for other developments.

Beginning at about the middle of the twentieth century two new trends in how to accomplish work started to coalesce. Many leaders recognized that the "science of management" was not enough, and many approaches to leadership were developed. While leaders from different walks of life continue to publish books on their secrets of success, students of leadership have been developing the discipline by looking for commonalities in the various schools of thought.

Project management is the second discipline that started to emerge in the middle of the twentieth century. People started to realize that planning, organizing, leading, and controlling one-time work efforts (projects) was not the same as for ongoing operations. The temporary nature and unique output of projects meant that they needed to be conducted in a different manner.

Both leadership and project management have become better defined—yet limited by their definitions. This has led to the desire to combine the knowledge and skills from the two distinct fields, and we call the combination project leadership.

Project leadership needs a framework, as does any other organized field. The project part of the framework is clear—we have introduced a four-stage project lifecycle model similar to those commonly used by project managers. The leadership aspect is a new challenge. We have distilled the many helpful ideas down to the seven major project leadership categories that must be performed during each of the four stages of a project's life for a total of 28 specific project leadership tasks.

There is both an art and a science to project leadership. The science is understanding what the project leadership responsibilities are at each point in the life of a project. What are the decisions that need to be made, which project leader(s) should make the decisions, and how are they connected to other project leadership responsibilities? The science also includes techniques that can be used to help project leaders make decisions, such as brainstorming, multi-voting, and consensus development.

The art of project leadership is the judgment or wisdom that can be developed to make the best decisions. Many project decisions are far from black and white. Many project decisions have implications for clients, workers, other participants, technology, money, time, etc. Both through experience and by studying project leadership as a discipline, the art can be developed.

In the rapidly changing world of today and tomorrow, an increasing number of people spend large amounts of time working on projects. People leading projects need to understand both the the science and the art of project leadership. The science is the identification of specific project leadership responsibilities at each project stage. The art includes understanding when to accept project realities and when to use courage in making difficult but necessary project decisions.

We encourage all project leaders—at whatever level they are—to thoughtfully consider the various project leadership challenges identified in this book, to relate them to the challenges they face on their projects, and to email us with their comments, suggestions, and examples. Good habits take time to fully develop. There are 28 specific challenges for project leaders. A leader who tries to apply one per week to his or her own work will make progress toward becoming a more effective project leader.

Project Leadership Assessment: Organizational

This questionnaire contains statements about the characteristics of an organization and how it is supportive and creates a culture that encourages project leadership. Rate each item on a five-point scale indicating whether you agree or disagree with the statement. There are no right or wrong answers. Mark one answer only for each question.

1 Senior management creates an environment and culture that nurtures the growth and development of project leaders and their teams.
❑ strongly disagree ❑ disagree ❑ neither disagree or agree ❑ agree ❑ strongly agree

2 Project leaders are encouraged to use vision to guide daily actions and decisions.
❑ strongly disagree ❑ disagree ❑ neither disagree or agree ❑ agree ❑ strongly agree

3 Decisions affecting the project are made after long, careful consideration.
❑ strongly disagree ❑ disagree ❑ neither disagree or agree ❑ agree ❑ strongly agree

4 There is a good relationship between the project team and senior management.
❑ strongly disagree ❑ disagree ❑ neither disagree or agree ❑ agree ❑ strongly agree

5 Risk should be avoided at all costs.
❑ strongly disagree ❑ disagree ❑ neither disagree or agree ❑ agree ❑ strongly agree

6 Project team members are treated with dignity and respect.
❑ strongly disagree ❑ disagree ❑ neither disagree or agree ❑ agree ❑ strongly agree

7 Environmental influences are monitored and controlled.
❑ strongly disagree ❑ disagree ❑ neither disagree or agree ❑ agree ❑ strongly agree

8 Conflict in the project team has a negative influence on successful performance.
❑ strongly disagree ❑ disagree ❑ neither disagree or agree ❑ agree ❑ strongly agree

9 Team members are encouraged to take initiative in problem-solving.
❑ strongly disagree ❑ disagree ❑ neither disagree or agree ❑ agree ❑ strongly agree

10 Senior management decisions are frequently reversed.
❑ strongly disagree ❑ disagree ❑ neither disagree or agree ❑ agree ❑ strongly agree

11 Organizational success is more important than resolving project team issues.
❏ strongly disagree ❏ disagree ❏ neither disagree or agree ❏ agree ❏ strongly agree

12 The singular focus of senior management is project results.
❏ strongly disagree ❏ disagree ❏ neither disagree or agree ❏ agree ❏ strongly agree

13 Changes in company strategy and project requirements are communicated and explained to team members.
❏ strongly disagree ❏ disagree ❏ neither disagree or agree ❏ agree ❏ strongly agree

14 A high degree of trust exists between senior management and project team members.
❏ strongly disagree ❏ disagree ❏ neither disagree or agree ❏ agree ❏ strongly agree

15 Leaders are encouraged to find creative solutions to business and project problems.
❏ strongly disagree ❏ disagree ❏ neither disagree or agree ❏ agree ❏ strongly agree

16 Teams are recognized and rewarded for good performance.
❏ strongly disagree ❏ disagree ❏ neither disagree or agree ❏ agree ❏ strongly agree

17 Project accomplishments are celebrated and shared with other project teams.
❏ strongly disagree ❏ disagree ❏ neither disagree or agree ❏ agree ❏ strongly agree

18 Change is a considered a way of life and necessary to organizational success.
❏ strongly disagree ❏ disagree ❏ neither disagree or agree ❏ agree ❏ strongly agree

19 Risk and problems are considered to be inherent in projects.
❏ strongly disagree ❏ disagree ❏ neither disagree or agree ❏ agree ❏ strongly agree

20 Authorization is a slow process due to complex and lengthy administrative procedures.
❏ strongly disagree ❏ disagree ❏ neither disagree or agree ❏ agree ❏ strongly agree

21 Senior management deals well with uncertainty.
❏ strongly disagree ❏ disagree ❏ neither disagree or agree ❏ agree ❏ strongly agree

22 Politics and power have a lot to do with project success.
❏ strongly disagree ❏ disagree ❏ neither disagree or agree ❏ agree ❏ strongly agree

23 Senior management has a customer satisfaction orientation and not just a profit motive.
❏ strongly disagree ❏ disagree ❏ neither disagree or agree ❏ agree ❏ strongly agree

24 Quality is an important factor in a successful project.
❏ strongly disagree ❏ disagree ❏ neither disagree or agree ❏ agree ❏ strongly agree

25 Trust and interdependence between all stakeholders are considered critical success factors.
❏ strongly disagree ❏ disagree ❏ neither disagree or agree ❏ agree ❏ strongly agree

26 Organizational policies and practices enable the project team to deliver according to plan.
❏ strongly disagree ❏ disagree ❏ neither disagree or agree ❏ agree ❏ strongly agree

27 Project mistakes and errors are dealt with in a positive and constructive manner.
❏ strongly disagree ❏ disagree ❏ neither disagree or agree ❏ agree ❏ strongly agree

28 Senior management members act as sponsors and champions that support and encourage high levels of project performance.
❏ strongly disagree ❏ disagree ❏ neither disagree or agree ❏ agree ❏ strongly agree

29 Concerns on the part of senior management are minimized and dealt with by frequent and open communications.
❏ strongly disagree ❏ disagree ❏ neither disagree or agree ❏ agree ❏ strongly agree

30 There is a high degree of trust among all of the stakeholders.
❏ strongly disagree ❏ disagree ❏ neither disagree or agree ❏ agree ❏ strongly agree

31 Organizational goals are more important than team or individual goals.
❏ strongly disagree ❏ disagree ❏ neither disagree or agree ❏ agree ❏ strongly agree

32 Stakeholders are prepared to take calculated risks.
❏ strongly disagree ❏ disagree ❏ neither disagree or agree ❏ agree ❏ strongly agree

33 Changes in the environment are discussed between senior management and project teams before decisions are made.
❏ strongly disagree ❏ disagree ❏ neither disagree or agree ❏ agree ❏ strongly agree

34 Senior management gets directly involved with the supervision of the project teams.
❏ strongly disagree ❏ disagree ❏ neither disagree or agree ❏ agree ❏ strongly agree

35 The organizational environment encourages creativity and innovation.
❏ strongly disagree ❏ disagree ❏ neither disagree or agree ❏ agree ❏ strongly agree

36 Management does not interfere with the decision-making process in project teams.
❏ strongly disagree ❏ disagree ❏ neither disagree or agree ❏ agree ❏ strongly agree

37 The organization protects its project teams against external influences.
❏ strongly disagree ❏ disagree ❏ neither disagree or agree ❏ agree ❏ strongly agree

38 The process for project management is clearly defined and communicated.
❏ strongly disagree ❏ disagree ❏ neither disagree or agree ❏ agree ❏ strongly agree

39 Senior management encourages calculated risk-taking.
❏ strongly disagree ❏ disagree ❏ neither disagree or agree ❏ agree ❏ strongly agree

40 Teamwork is important for project success.
❏ strongly disagree ❏ disagree ❏ neither disagree or agree ❏ agree ❏ strongly agree

41 Using a formalized project methodology and tools is important for project success.
❏ strongly disagree ❏ disagree ❏ neither disagree or agree ❏ agree ❏ strongly agree

42 The success of the organization and the success of the project teams are intertwined.
❏ strongly disagree ❏ disagree ❏ neither disagree or agree ❏ agree ❏ strongly agree

43 The project management process supports tracking the accomplishment of deliverables.
❏ strongly disagree ❏ disagree ❏ neither disagree or agree ❏ agree ❏ strongly agree

44 Meetings and communications requests increase significantly in times of project crisis.
❏ strongly disagree ❏ disagree ❏ neither disagree or agree ❏ agree ❏ strongly agree

45 The organization conducts its business in an ethical manner.
❏ strongly disagree ❏ disagree ❏ neither disagree or agree ❏ agree ❏ strongly agree

46 The progress of the projects is carefully and systematically monitored by management.
❏ strongly disagree ❏ disagree ❏ neither disagree or agree ❏ agree ❏ strongly agree

47 Project corrective actions are taken proactively and in a positive manner.
❏ strongly disagree ❏ disagree ❏ neither disagree or agree ❏ agree ❏ strongly agree

48 Senior management follows a decentralized approach in decision-making.
❏ strongly disagree ❏ disagree ❏ neither disagree or agree ❏ agree ❏ strongly agree

49 The organization recognizes the importance of the interpersonal aspects of project leadership.
❏ strongly disagree ❏ disagree ❏ neither disagree or agree ❏ agree ❏ strongly agree

50 The organization sets a climate and environment for leadership to flourish by clear policies, guidance, and direction as well as visible and vocal support for the leaders and the projects.
❏ strongly disagree ❏ disagree ❏ neither disagree or agree ❏ agree ❏ strongly agree

Scoring

The scoring for this questionnaire is divided into six groups: Cultural, Teamwork and Interpersonal, Risk, Communications, Decision-making and Problem-solving, and Trust and Interdependence. The scores for these groupings will provide some initial insight into the organizational aspects of project leadership and are to be used as a guide to further analysis and evaluation.

Cultural

This grouping of questions relates to the cultural aspects of leadership or how well the organization supports leaders and the development of leadership skills.

Score questions 1, 7, 18, 23, 24, 26, 28, 35, 37, 41, 43, 46, and 50 on the scale below:

1 = strongly disagree 2 = disagree 3 = neither disagree or agree 4 = agree 5 = strongly agree

Score questions 11, 12, 22, and 31 on the scale below:

5 = strongly disagree 4 = disagree 3 = neither disagree or agree 2 = agree 1 = strongly agree

Add the individual scores for these questions and divide the total score for this group by 17.

Teamwork and Interpersonal

This grouping of questions relates to the aspects of leadership associated with teamwork and the interpersonal aspects of teams and projects.

Score questions 4, 6, 16, 17, 40, and 49 on the scale below:

1 = strongly disagree 2 = disagree 3 = neither disagree or agree 4 = agree 5 = strongly agree

Score question 8 on the scale below:

5 = strongly disagree 4 = disagree 3 = neither disagree or agree 2 = agree 1 = strongly agree

Add the individual scores for these questions and divide the total score for this group by 7.

Risk

This grouping of questions relates to risk and the organization's willingness to address risk related to projects.

Score questions 19, 21, 32, and 39 on the scale below:

1 = strongly disagree 2 = disagree 3 = neither disagree or agree 4 = agree 5 = strongly agree

Score question 5 on the scale below:

5 = strongly disagree 4 = disagree 3 = neither disagree or agree 2 = agree 1 = strongly agree

Add the individual scores for these questions and divide the total score for this group by 5.

Communications

This grouping of questions relates to communications within organizations, with stakeholders, and between senior management and the project teams.

Score questions 13, 29, and 38 on the scale below:

1 = strongly disagree 2 = disagree 3 = neither disagree or agree 4 = agree 5 = strongly agree

Score question 44 on the scale below:

5 = strongly disagree 4 = disagree 3 = neither disagree or agree 2 = agree 1 = strongly agree

Add the individual scores for these questions and divide the total score for this group by 4.

Decision-making and Problem-solving

This grouping of questions relates to decision-making and problem-solving in the organizations and senior management's willingness to allow leaders and teams to be involved in these processes.

Score questions 2, 9, 15, 33, 36, and 48 on the scale below:

1 = strongly disagree 2 = disagree 3 = neither disagree or agree 4 = agree 5 = strongly agree

Score questions 3, 10, and 20 on the scale below:

5 = strongly disagree 4 = disagree 3 = neither disagree or agree 2 = agree 1 = strongly agree

Add the individual scores for these questions and divide the total score for this group by 9.

Trust and Interdependence

This grouping of questions relates to trust and interdependence within project teams, within organizations, and between project teams and stakeholders.

Score questions 14, 25, 30, 42, 45, and 47 on the scale below:

1 = strongly disagree 2 = disagree 3 = neither disagree or agree 4 = agree 5 = strongly agree

Score question 34 on the scale below:

5 = strongly disagree 4 = disagree 3 = neither disagree or agree 2 = agree 1 = strongly agree

Add the individual scores for these questions and divide the total score for this group by 7.

Interpretation

The following are average scores for the above groupings:

0.0–3.0   The organization is not providing a cultural environment that is conducive to effective project leadership.

3.1–3.9   The organization demonstrates some characteristics and attributes that are conducive to effective leadership, but has room for growth and improvement.

4.0–5.0   The organization is providing a cultural atmosphere and professional environment that is encouraging and supportive for effective project leadership.

Project Leadership Assessment: Individual

This questionnaire contains statements about the individual characteristics of a project leader. Rate each item on a five-point scale indicating whether you agree or disagree with the statement. There are no right or wrong answers. Mark one answer only for each question:

1 I am able to develop and enthusiastically communicate a vision for the project to the team.
   ❏ strongly disagree   ❏ disagree   ❏ neither disagree or agree   ❏ agree   ❏ strongly agree

2 Conflict within a project team can be a good thing.
   ❏ strongly disagree   ❏ disagree   ❏ neither disagree or agree   ❏ agree   ❏ strongly agree

3 Risk should be avoided at all costs.
   ❏ strongly disagree   ❏ disagree   ❏ neither disagree or agree   ❏ agree   ❏ strongly agree

4 All corporate policies and procedures should be followed.
   ❏ strongly disagree   ❏ disagree   ❏ neither disagree or agree   ❏ agree   ❏ strongly agree

5 Conflict is a negative influence on the success of a project.
   ❏ strongly disagree   ❏ disagree   ❏ neither disagree or agree   ❏ agree   ❏ strongly agree

6 Team members are encouraged to take initiative in problem solving.
   ❏ strongly disagree   ❏ disagree   ❏ neither disagree or agree   ❏ agree   ❏ strongly agree

7 The primary focus of the project is on results.
   ❏ strongly disagree   ❏ disagree   ❏ neither disagree or agree   ❏ agree   ❏ strongly agree

8 I have the ability to look forward, see the big picture, and effectively communicate that to stakeholders and team members.
   ❏ strongly disagree   ❏ disagree   ❏ neither disagree or agree   ❏ agree   ❏ strongly agree

9 Project success is more important than resolving individual issues.
   ❏ strongly disagree   ❏ disagree   ❏ neither disagree or agree   ❏ agree   ❏ strongly agree

10 I have the ability to build multi-functional teams.
    ❏ strongly disagree   ❏ disagree   ❏ neither disagree or agree   ❏ agree   ❏ strongly agree

11 Rewarding and recognizing team members for good performance increases motivation.
❏ strongly disagree ❏ disagree ❏ neither disagree or agree ❏ agree ❏ strongly agree

12 I see uncertainty and problems as hindrances to project success.
❏ strongly disagree ❏ disagree ❏ neither disagree or agree ❏ agree ❏ strongly agree

13 I can clearly visualize the project process.
❏ strongly disagree ❏ disagree ❏ neither disagree or agree ❏ agree ❏ strongly agree

14 The project manager's leadership helps achieve project results.
❏ strongly disagree ❏ disagree ❏ neither disagree or agree ❏ agree ❏ strongly agree

15 I see myself as a facilitator or "broker" for change.
❏ strongly disagree ❏ disagree ❏ neither disagree or agree ❏ agree ❏ strongly agree

16 I have the ability to plan and elicit commitments.
❏ strongly disagree ❏ disagree ❏ neither disagree or agree ❏ agree ❏ strongly agree

17 Risk is monitored on a continuous basis.
❏ strongly disagree ❏ disagree ❏ neither disagree or agree ❏ agree ❏ strongly agree

18 Politics and power are managed as part of the project.
❏ strongly disagree ❏ disagree ❏ neither disagree or agree ❏ agree ❏ strongly agree

19 Customer expectations are clearly defined.
❏ strongly disagree ❏ disagree ❏ neither disagree or agree ❏ agree ❏ strongly agree

20 I view problems, issues, and uncertainty as challenges that can be overcome.
❏ strongly disagree ❏ disagree ❏ neither disagree or agree ❏ agree ❏ strongly agree

21 Progress assessment is done on a routine basis.
❏ strongly disagree ❏ disagree ❏ neither disagree or agree ❏ agree ❏ strongly agree

22 The project is clearly outlined with a work breakdown structure, definite start and ending dates, and a financial budget.
❏ strongly disagree ❏ disagree ❏ neither disagree or agree ❏ agree ❏ strongly agree

23 The project manager is responsible for meeting the schedule deadlines.
❏ strongly disagree ❏ disagree ❏ neither disagree or agree ❏ agree ❏ strongly agree

24 I am able to recognize the interdependence among stakeholders.
❏ strongly disagree ❏ disagree ❏ neither disagree or agree ❏ agree ❏ strongly agree

25 Stakeholder expectations have been clearly defined at the outset of the project.
❏ strongly disagree ❏ disagree ❏ neither disagree or agree ❏ agree ❏ strongly agree

26 Project failures, problems, and mistakes are openly discussed with senior management.
❏ strongly disagree ❏ disagree ❏ neither disagree or agree ❏ agree ❏ strongly agree

27 My individual performance is evaluated solely based on meeting the project goals.
❏ strongly disagree ❏ disagree ❏ neither disagree or agree ❏ agree ❏ strongly agree

28 I actively listen to different points of view.
❏ strongly disagree ❏ disagree ❏ neither disagree or agree ❏ agree ❏ strongly agree

29 I have the ability to collect and filter relevant data needed for decision-making.
❏ strongly disagree ❏ disagree ❏ neither disagree or agree ❏ agree ❏ strongly agree

30 Short and informal lines of communication are used.
❏ strongly disagree ❏ disagree ❏ neither disagree or agree ❏ agree ❏ strongly agree

31 Organizational policies and practices enable the project to deliver according to plan.
❏ strongly disagree ❏ disagree ❏ neither disagree or agree ❏ agree ❏ strongly agree

32 The work breakdown structure is used to determine the selection of the team members based on skills and knowledge required.
❑ strongly disagree ❑ disagree ❑ neither disagree or agree ❑ agree ❑ strongly agree

33 I am able to adapt to different circumstances and a changing environment.
❑ strongly disagree ❑ disagree ❑ neither disagree or agree ❑ agree ❑ strongly agree

34 Expectations are set and concerns minimized by enthusiastically distributing information to all stakeholders.
❑ strongly disagree ❑ disagree ❑ neither disagree or agree ❑ agree ❑ strongly agree

35 I keep my commitments and promises.
❑ strongly disagree ❑ disagree ❑ neither disagree or agree ❑ agree ❑ strongly agree

36 I have a good working relationship with the customer and other stakeholders.
❑ strongly disagree ❑ disagree ❑ neither disagree or agree ❑ agree ❑ strongly agree

37 Using a project methodology, tools, and techniques is important for project success.
❑ strongly disagree ❑ disagree ❑ neither disagree or agree ❑ agree ❑ strongly agree

38 Problems and uncertainty are dealt with through open communication.
❑ strongly disagree ❑ disagree ❑ neither disagree or agree ❑ agree ❑ strongly agree

39 I am able to secure the resources needed to successfully complete the project.
❑ strongly disagree ❑ disagree ❑ neither disagree or agree ❑ agree ❑ strongly agree

40 I have control of the resources necessary to successfully complete the project.
❑ strongly disagree ❑ disagree ❑ neither disagree or agree ❑ agree ❑ strongly agree

41 I have daily communication with the project team members.
❑ strongly disagree ❑ disagree ❑ neither disagree or agree ❑ agree ❑ strongly agree

42 The project team members can count on me to assist them to be successful.
❑ strongly disagree ❑ disagree ❑ neither disagree or agree ❑ agree ❑ strongly agree

43 I like to manage the tasks one at a time to ensure we stay on track.
❑ strongly disagree ❑ disagree ❑ neither disagree or agree ❑ agree ❑ strongly agree

44 Project meetings always have an agenda, have minutes documented, and identify actions, responsibilities, and timeframes.
❑ strongly disagree ❑ disagree ❑ neither disagree or agree ❑ agree ❑ strongly agree

45 I conduct business in an honest and ethical manner.
❑ strongly disagree ❑ disagree ❑ neither disagree or agree ❑ agree ❑ strongly agree

46 I have a good professional reputation and a track record of project success.
❑ strongly disagree ❑ disagree ❑ neither disagree or agree ❑ agree ❑ strongly agree

47 My personal values include the appreciation of all peoples and groups.
❑ strongly disagree ❑ disagree ❑ neither disagree or agree ❑ agree ❑ strongly agree

48 I have a good relationship with senior management, stakeholders, and members of industry, which creates an atmosphere of mutual trust and respect.
❑ strongly disagree ❑ disagree ❑ neither disagree or agree ❑ agree ❑ strongly agree

49 I have the ability to deal effectively with managers and support personnel across functional lines, often with little or no formal authority.
❑ strongly disagree ❑ disagree ❑ neither disagree or agree ❑ agree ❑ strongly agree

50 I have the ability to integrate individual demands, requirements, and limitations into decisions that benefit the overall project.
❑ strongly disagree ❑ disagree ❑ neither disagree or agree ❑ agree ❑ strongly agree

Scoring

The scoring for this questionnaire is divided into six groups: Team-building and Interpersonal; Planning and Risk; Communications; Decision-making, Problem-solving, and Performance; Trust and Interdependence; and Cultural and Environmental. The scores for these groupings will provide some initial insight into the individual aspects of leadership and are to be used as a guide to further analysis and evaluation.

Team-building and Interpersonal

This grouping of questions relates to the aspects of leadership related to team-building and the interpersonal aspects of teams and projects.

Score questions 2, 10, 11, 16, 45, and 47 on the scale below:

1 = strongly disagree 2 = disagree 3 = neither disagree or agree 4 = agree 5 = strongly agree

Score question 5 on the scale below:

5 = strongly disagree 4 = disagree 3 = neither disagree or agree 2 = agree 1 = strongly agree

Add the individual scores for these questions and divide the total score for this group by 7.

Planning and Risk

This grouping of questions relates to planning and risk and the organization's and team's willingness to address project-related risk.

Score questions 13, 17, 22, 32, and 39 on the scale below:

1 = strongly disagree 2 = disagree 3 = neither disagree or agree 4 = agree 5 = strongly agree

Score question 3 on the scale below:

5 = strongly disagree 4 = disagree 3 = neither disagree or agree 2 = agree 1 = strongly agree

Add the individual scores for these questions and divide the total score for this group by 6.

Communications

This grouping of questions relates to communications within organizations, with stakeholders, and between senior management and project teams.

Score questions 1, 8, 19, 28, 34, 41, and 44 on the scale below:

1 = strongly disagree 2 = disagree 3 = neither disagree or agree 4 = agree 5 = strongly agree

Score question 30 on the scale below:
5 = strongly disagree 4 = disagree 3 = neither disagree or agree 2 = agree 1 = strongly agree

Add the individual scores for these questions and divide the total score for this group by 8.

Decision-making, Problem-solving, and Performance

This grouping of questions relates to decision-making, problem-solving and project performance.

Score questions 6, 7, 14, 20, 21, 23, 29, 46, 49, and 50 on the scale below:
1 = strongly disagree 2 = disagree 3 = neither disagree or agree 4 = agree 5 = strongly agree

Score questions 9, 12, 26, 27, and 43 on the scale below:
5 = strongly disagree 4 = disagree 3 = neither disagree or agree 2 = agree 1 = strongly agree

Add the individual scores for these questions and divide the total score for this group by 15.

Trust and Interdependence

This grouping of questions relates to trust and interdependence within project teams, within organizations, and between project teams and stakeholders.

Score questions 24, 25, 36, 42, and 48 on the scale below:
1 = strongly disagree 2 = disagree 3 = neither disagree or agree 4 = agree 5 = strongly agree

Score question 38 on the scale below:
5 = strongly disagree 4 = disagree 3 = neither disagree or agree 2 = agree 1 = strongly agree

Add the individual scores for these questions and divide the total score for this group by 6.

Cultural and Environmental

This grouping of questions relates to the cultural and environmental aspects of leadership.

Score questions 4, 15, 31, 33, 35, and 37 on the scale below:
1 = strongly disagree 2 = disagree 3 = neither disagree or agree 4 = agree 5 = strongly agree

Score questions 18 and 40 on the scale below:
5 = strongly disagree 4 = disagree 3 = neither disagree or agree 2 = agree 1 = strongly agree

Add the individual scores for these questions and divide the total score for this group by 8.

Interpretation

The following are average scores for the above groupings:

0.0–3.0   The individual leadership characteristics and attributes identified do not indicate effective leadership is being demonstrated and that leadership development is required.

3.1–3.9   The individual leadership characteristics and attributes identified have some aspects associated with effective leadership, but there is room for growth and improvement.

4.0–5.0   Effective individual leadership characteristics and attributes are being demonstrated.

Project Leadership Assessment: Team

This questionnaire contains statements about the team aspects of project leadership. Rate each item on a five-point scale indicating whether you agree or disagree with the statement. There are no right or wrong answers. Mark one answer only for each question.

1   The project team actively participates in project planning.
❏ strongly disagree ❏ disagree ❏ neither disagree or agree ❏ agree ❏ strongly agree

2   Project team members are treated with dignity and respect.
❏ strongly disagree ❏ disagree ❏ neither disagree or agree ❏ agree ❏ strongly agree

3   The project team members are recognized and rewarded for their contributions.
❏ strongly disagree ❏ disagree ❏ neither disagree or agree ❏ agree ❏ strongly agree

4   Tasks are not broken down into work packages that are clearly communicated to the project team members.
❏ strongly disagree ❏ disagree ❏ neither disagree or agree ❏ agree ❏ strongly agree

5   The project team is not kept informed of all of the details regarding the status of the project.
❏ strongly disagree ❏ disagree ❏ neither disagree or agree ❏ agree ❏ strongly agree

6   Conflict within project teams is recognized as a problem and is dealt with in a timely manner.
❏ strongly disagree ❏ disagree ❏ neither disagree or agree ❏ agree ❏ strongly agree

7   Team members are encouraged to find innovative ways to improve project performance.
❏ strongly disagree ❏ disagree ❏ neither disagree or agree ❏ agree ❏ strongly agree

8   Kickoff meetings are used to initially inform project team members of their responsibilities and how their work relates to the "big picture."
❏ strongly disagree ❏ disagree ❏ neither disagree or agree ❏ agree ❏ strongly agree

9   Team spirit and high morale among the team members are maintained by group activities and open communications.
❏ strongly disagree ❏ disagree ❏ neither disagree or agree ❏ agree ❏ strongly agree

10   Decision-making is performed quickly and in a participative manner.
❏ strongly disagree ❏ disagree ❏ neither disagree or agree ❏ agree ❏ strongly agree

11   Project team members are encouraged to take initiative in solving problems.
❏ strongly disagree ❏ disagree ❏ neither disagree or agree ❏ agree ❏ strongly agree

12   The project team members trust and look to the leader for guidance and support.
❏ strongly disagree ❏ disagree ❏ neither disagree or agree ❏ agree ❏ strongly agree

13 There is a high degree of trust between senior management and project team members.
❏ strongly disagree   ❏ disagree   ❏ neither disagree or agree   ❏ agree   ❏ strongly agree

14 The relationship between project team members is positive and cooperative.
❏ strongly disagree   ❏ disagree   ❏ neither disagree or agree   ❏ agree   ❏ strongly agree

15 There is a strong sense of belonging between the project team members.
❏ strongly disagree   ❏ disagree   ❏ neither disagree or agree   ❏ agree   ❏ strongly agree

16 The project team pulls together in times of adversity to find solutions to problems.
❏ strongly disagree   ❏ disagree   ❏ neither disagree or agree   ❏ agree   ❏ strongly agree

17 The project team members are dedicated and deliver their tasks on schedule and with quality.
❏ strongly disagree   ❏ disagree   ❏ neither disagree or agree   ❏ agree   ❏ strongly agree

18 The project vision and process are clearly communicated to the team.
❏ strongly disagree   ❏ disagree   ❏ neither disagree or agree   ❏ agree   ❏ strongly agree

19 Each project team member takes responsibility to monitor risk and inform the leader when risk triggers or events are detected.
❏ strongly disagree   ❏ disagree   ❏ neither disagree or agree   ❏ agree   ❏ strongly agree

20 The project team maintains high quality throughout the project lifecycle.
❏ strongly disagree   ❏ disagree   ❏ neither disagree or agree   ❏ agree   ❏ strongly agree

21 The project team has a high level of orientation toward customer satisfaction.
❏ strongly disagree   ❏ disagree   ❏ neither disagree or agree   ❏ agree   ❏ strongly agree

22 The team routinely meets project budgets and schedules.
❏ strongly disagree   ❏ disagree   ❏ neither disagree or agree   ❏ agree   ❏ strongly agree

23 Conflict within the project team is a destructive force that must be eliminated.
❏ strongly disagree   ❏ disagree   ❏ neither disagree or agree   ❏ agree   ❏ strongly agree

24 The team members understand the project's strategic importance and their stake in the project's success.
❏ strongly disagree   ❏ disagree   ❏ neither disagree or agree   ❏ agree   ❏ strongly agree

25 The policies and practices that apply to the project are clearly understood and strictly followed by all team members.
❏ strongly disagree   ❏ disagree   ❏ neither disagree or agree   ❏ agree   ❏ strongly agree

26 Team performance is evaluated based on the project goals.
❏ strongly disagree   ❏ disagree   ❏ neither disagree or agree   ❏ agree   ❏ strongly agree

27 Mistakes and errors are resolved in a positive and solution-oriented way.
❏ strongly disagree   ❏ disagree   ❏ neither disagree or agree   ❏ agree   ❏ strongly agree

28 The team members are carefully selected by the project leader for the project.
❏ strongly disagree   ❏ disagree   ❏ neither disagree or agree   ❏ agree   ❏ strongly agree

29 Project team members have the courage to view criticism in a positive and open manner.
❏ strongly disagree   ❏ disagree   ❏ neither disagree or agree   ❏ agree   ❏ strongly agree

30 The project team celebrates accomplishments.
❏ strongly disagree   ❏ disagree   ❏ neither disagree or agree   ❏ agree   ❏ strongly agree

31 The project team minimizes uncertainty and concern by distributing information to all stakeholders.
❏ strongly disagree   ❏ disagree   ❏ neither disagree or agree   ❏ agree   ❏ strongly agree

32 The project team sets clearly defined goals, makes detailed plans, and has established, attainable milestones.
❑ strongly disagree   ❑ disagree   ❑ neither disagree or agree   ❑ agree   ❑ strongly agree

33 The team members work in an atmosphere of mutual respect and trust.
❑ strongly disagree   ❑ disagree   ❑ neither disagree or agree   ❑ agree   ❑ strongly agree

34 The project team lacks a sense of shared enthusiasm for the project.
❑ strongly disagree   ❑ disagree   ❑ neither disagree or agree   ❑ agree   ❑ strongly agree

35 The project team is a cohesive group that is fully committed to the project.
❑ strongly disagree   ❑ disagree   ❑ neither disagree or agree   ❑ agree   ❑ strongly agree

36 The project team does not have good rapport with functional departments and vendors.
❑ strongly disagree   ❑ disagree   ❑ neither disagree or agree   ❑ agree   ❑ strongly agree

37 Both technical and interpersonal training is provided for the team.
❑ strongly disagree   ❑ disagree   ❑ neither disagree or agree   ❑ agree   ❑ strongly agree

38 The team leader is concerned about the development and well being of the team members.
❑ strongly disagree   ❑ disagree   ❑ neither disagree or agree   ❑ agree   ❑ strongly agree

39 Using project methodology and tools is important for project success
❑ strongly disagree   ❑ disagree   ❑ neither disagree or agree   ❑ agree   ❑ strongly agree

40 The team has open and frequent communication with the team leader.
❑ strongly disagree   ❑ disagree   ❑ neither disagree or agree   ❑ agree   ❑ strongly agree

41 Senior management provides the team with resources and support.
❑ strongly disagree   ❑ disagree   ❑ neither disagree or agree   ❑ agree   ❑ strongly agree

42 The project team does not have the authority to make decisions.
❑ strongly disagree   ❑ disagree   ❑ neither disagree or agree   ❑ agree   ❑ strongly agree

43 Project team members do not take personal responsibility to ensure schedules are met.
❑ strongly disagree   ❑ disagree   ❑ neither disagree or agree   ❑ agree   ❑ strongly agree

44 Project team members help one another and look out for each other's best interests.
❑ strongly disagree   ❑ disagree   ❑ neither disagree or agree   ❑ agree   ❑ strongly agree

45 Project teams are not able to respond immediately to changes in requirements or the project environment.
❑ strongly disagree   ❑ disagree   ❑ neither disagree or agree   ❑ agree   ❑ strongly agree

46 The project leader's style is adaptive to the different project phases and the needs of the team.
❑ strongly disagree   ❑ disagree   ❑ neither disagree or agree   ❑ agree   ❑ strongly agree

47 The project team leader has a good relationship with senior management.
❑ strongly disagree   ❑ disagree   ❑ neither disagree or agree   ❑ agree   ❑ strongly agree

48 The project team members are punished for failure to meet project objectives.
❑ strongly disagree   ❑ disagree   ❑ neither disagree or agree   ❑ agree   ❑ strongly agree

49 Each team member is clear about his or her role and responsibilities in the project.
❑ strongly disagree   ❑ disagree   ❑ neither disagree or agree   ❑ agree   ❑ strongly agree

50 The team has confidence in the team leader and trusts his or her judgment.
❑ strongly disagree   ❑ disagree   ❑ neither disagree or agree   ❑ agree   ❑ strongly agree

Scoring

The scoring for this questionnaire is divided into six groups: Planning, Teamwork and Interpersonal, Communications, Decision-making and Problem-solving, Trust and Interdependence, and Team Performance. The scores for these groupings will provide some initial insight into the team aspects of project leadership and are to be used as a guide for further analysis and evaluation.

Planning

This grouping of questions relates to the aspects of team leadership related to project planning.

Score questions 1, 28, and 32 on the scale below:

1 = strongly disagree 2 = disagree 3 = neither disagree or agree 4 = agree 5 = strongly agree

Score question 4 on the scale below:

5 = strongly disagree 4 = disagree 3 = neither disagree or agree 2 = agree 1 = strongly agree

Add the individual scores for these questions and divide the total score for this group by 4.

Teamwork and Interpersonal

This grouping of questions relates to the aspects of leadership associated with teamwork and team interpersonal aspects.

Score questions 2, 3, 9, 16, 27, 30, 35, 37, 38, 41, and 44 on the scale below:

1 = strongly disagree 2 = disagree 3 = neither disagree or agree 4 = agree 5 = strongly agree

Score questions 6, 23, 36, and 45 on the scale below:

5 = strongly disagree 4 = disagree 3 = neither disagree or agree 2 = agree 1 = strongly agree

Add the individual scores for these questions and divide the total score for this group by 15.

Communications

This grouping of questions relates to communications within organizations, with stakeholders, and between senior management and the project teams.

Score questions 8, 18, 24, 31, 40, and 49 on the scale below:

1 = strongly disagree 2 = disagree 3 = neither disagree or agree 4 = agree 5 = strongly agree

Score questions 5 and 25 on the scale below:

5 = strongly disagree 4 = disagree 3 = neither disagree or agree 2 = agree 1 = strongly agree

Add the individual scores for these questions and divide the total score for this group by 8.

Decision-making and Problem-solving

This grouping of questions relates to decision making and problem solving in the organization and senior management's willingness to allow leaders and teams to be involved in these processes.

Score questions 10 and 11 on the scale below:

1 = strongly disagree 2 = disagree 3 = neither disagree or agree 4 = agree 5 = strongly agree

Score question 42 on the scale below:

5 = strongly disagree 4 = disagree 3 = neither disagree or agree 2 = agree 1 = strongly agree

Add the individual scores for these questions and divide the total score for this group by 3.

Trust and Interdependence

This grouping of questions relates to trust and interdependence within project teams, within the organization, and between project teams and stakeholders.

Score questions 12, 13, 14, 15, 29, 33, 47, and 50 on the scale below:

1 = strongly disagree 2 = disagree 3 = neither disagree or agree 4 = agree 5 = strongly agree

Score question 34 on the scale below:

5 = strongly disagree 4 = disagree 3 = neither disagree or agree 2 = agree 1 = strongly agree

Add the individual scores for these questions and divide the total score for this group by 9.

Team Performance

This grouping of questions relates to team performance.

Score questions 7, 17, 19, 20, 21, 22, 26, 39, and 46 on the scale below:

1 = strongly disagree 2 = disagree 3 = neither disagree or agree 4 = agree 5 = strongly agree

Score questions 43 and 48 on the scale below:

5 = strongly disagree 4 = disagree 3 = neither disagree or agree 2 = agree 1 = strongly agree

Add the individual scores for these questions and divide the total score for this group by 11.

Interpretation

The following are average scores for the above groupings:

0.0–3.0   The project team and its leadership is not as effective as it should be and both leadership development and team member development are required.

3.1–3.9   The project team demonstrates some aspects and characteristics of effective leadership, but has room for growth and improvement.

4.0–5.0   The project team is functioning effectively in a professional environment that demonstrates the characteristic and attributes of effective project leadership.

Glossary

Administrative closure	Generating, gathering, and disseminating information to formalize phase or project completion.
Administrative principles	A subfield of the classical management perspective that focuses on the total organization rather than the individual worker, delineating the management functions of planning, controlling, organizing, commanding, and coordinating.
Agenda	A list or program of things to be done or considered for a meeting. A meeting agenda typically contains the purpose of the meeting, date, time, place, and topics to be discussed in the meeting.
Align	The act of bringing a project vision into proper or desirable coordination with the parent organization's vision.
Authorize work	Ordering of project activities to commence.
Available to promise document	One of the documents created in the supply chain process to indicate the availability of materials and promise to deliver on a date.
Behavioral sciences approach	A subfield of the humanistic management perspective that applies social science in an organizational context.
Brainstorm	A group of people working together to generate ideas.
Budget, project budget	A plan for allocating resources. A means to measure the difference between actual and estimated project cost. WBS costed in a step-by-step fashion.
Bureaucratic organizations	A classical management perspective that emphasizes management based on clearly defined authority and responsibility along with separation of management and ownership.
Business analyst	A programmer or consultant who designs and manages the development of business applications. Typically more involved in design issues than in day-to-day coding.
Business case	The business reason or value for undertaking the project.
Business to business	The exchange of products, services, or information between businesses rather than between businesses and consumers. Also known as B2B or e-biz.
Buy-in	An informal and internalized commitment to an idea or project.
Celebrate	Festive commemoration at the end of project or major project component.
Change control plan	A process for approval of modifications, additions, and deletions to the project baseline.
Change management	The disciplined use of a defined process to control project modifications, additions, and deletions.

Change request document, change order form	A form used to capture modifications, additions, and deletions to project scope that may impact schedule, budget, or other work.
Collaborate	To work together, especially in a joint intellectual effort.
Commit	The act of pledging to accomplish work and being determined to do whatever it takes to accomplish the work.
Communication and control plan	Action plan that determines the information and communication needs of all stakeholders (who needs what information, when they will need it, and how it will be given to them).
Complementary metal-oxide semiconductor (CMOS)	The dominant semiconductor technology for microprocessors, memories, and application-specific integrated circuits.
Conceptual skill	The cognitive ability to see the organization as a whole and the relationships among its parts.
Configuration	The details of how the system is structured.
Conflict management	Resolution of disagreements and tensions.
Consensus	A decision-making method by which every single person on the project team agrees that the decision makes sense and he or she will enthusiastically support it.
Contingency plan	An identification of alternative strategies to be used to ensure project success if specified risk events occur.
Contingency view	An extension of the humanistic perspective in which successful resolution of organizational problems is thought to depend on managers' identification of key variables in the situation at hand.
Control	The process of comparing actual performance with planned performance, analyzing variances, evaluating possible alternatives, and taking appropriate corrective action as needed.
Coordinate	To harmonize in a common action or effort. Project managers often need to coordinate the efforts of various workers from different disciplines over whom they have no authority.
Core team	The small group who will collectively make many project decisions and perform many of the project's tasks, ideally assigned to the project from start to finish.
Corrective action	The process of returning some aspect of project performance to a more desired state.
Critical success factors	A brief listing of what should be monitored closely on an ongoing basis to ensure that the project is proceeding adequately. Also known as the project vital signs or metrics.
Customer	Someone for whom work or service is performed, both external to and internal within the organization.
Decision-making	The process of making choices in a project team environment. Several types of decision-making are useful in projects: consensus, leader-imposed, delegated, voting, and scoring models.
Delegate	To commit or entrust responsibility to another.
Detailed plan/ detailed project plan	The in-depth method of simultaneously accomplishing the scope, activities, resources, communication, and budget goals of the project.
Discipline	Control gained by a determined effort to follow both formal and informal methods that have proven to be effective.

DRAM	Dynamic Random Access Memory.
Duration	The number of work periods required to complete an activity or other project element.
Earned value	Percentage of the actual work accomplished compared to the work planned for each WBS element.
Economic forces	Forces that affect the availability, production, and distribution of a society's resources.
Effective	A customer's view of the usefulness of the project deliverables.
Efficient	Exhibiting a high ratio of output to input.
Empower	Enabling followers to take responsibility for actions.
Enterprise resource planning (ERP)	An industry term for the broad set of activities supported by multi-module application software that helps a manufacturer or other business manage the important parts of its business, including product planning, parts purchasing, maintaining inventories, interacting with suppliers, providing customer service, and tracking orders.
Excite	To arouse strong feeling in an unofficial commitment and to have fun in anticipation of official commitment; to boost the morale of the team and make them believe that their project work is important.
Executing stage/ project executing	The third of the four stages in the project lifecycle model. The time when most of the actual hands-on project work is accomplished and most of the money is spent, as plans are implemented.
Executive team	Top executive and his or her direct reports who collectively make many organizational decisions.
Fabrication	In semiconductor manufacturing, the front-end process of making devices and integrated circuits in semiconductor wafers; does not include the package assembly (back-end) stages.
Facilitator	One who contributes structure and process to interactions so groups are able to function effectively and make high-quality decisions. A helper and enabler whose goal is to support others as they achieve exceptional performance.
Fab	Fabrication facility, a silicon wafer manufacturing plant.
Freeze	End the additions and updates.
Functional specifications	The details of how a process should work in an organization for a business process without technical details.
Functional structure/divisional structure	A method of organizing in which common specialties are grouped into homogenous units.
Group dynamics	Skill and knowledge needed to help team members process diverse viewpoints.
Human relations movement	A movement in management thinking and practice that emphasizes the satisfaction of employees' basic needs as the key to increased worker productivity.
Human skill	The ability to work with and through other people and to work efficiently as a group member.
Humanistic perspective	A management perspective that emphasizes human behavior, needs, and attitudes.
Implementation	Carrying out of planned activity.
Inform	To make aware of.

Initiating stage/ project initiating	Authorizing the project or phase.
Integrate	To make into a whole by bringing all parts together.
Integrated circuit (IC)	A circuit in which active and passive electronic elements are fabricated and interconnected on a substrate.
Integrated project plan	Entire project plan, including the project charter, team charter, WBS, schedule, risk plan, and cost estimates.
Internal customers	Stakeholders of the project within an organization.
Justify project	To prove the importance of the project.
Key project participants	The people responsible for the project, specifically the project sponsor, project manager, steering team, and core team.
Key stakeholder	Someone who has a strong interest in making the project succeed because he or she is affected by the activities or the deliverables of the project.
Key stakeholder approval	Favorable opinion provided by key stakeholders so that the project can proceed after it has met their expectations.
Leader	One who leads or guides.
Leader-imposed	Decisions made by project leaders. Some project decisions must conform to organizational desires. Since the project leaders (especially the sponsor and the project manager) are often in the best position to understand the organization, they should make the decision and inform the team. Those decisions are leader-imposed.
Leading	The management function that energizes people to contribute their best individually and in cooperation with other people.
Learning organization	The management approach based on an organization anticipating faster than its counterparts and thus having an advantage in the market over its competitors, with emphasis on identifying problems as quickly as possible, correcting them, removing the underlying causes, and learning from them so that they do not reappear.
Legacy system	Systems that have been inherited from languages, platforms, and techniques earlier than current technology.
Lessons learned	The learning gained from the process of performing the project. Lessons learned may be identified at any point. Also considered a project record.
Management information system (MIS)	A system created specifically to store and provide information to managers.
Management science	One branch of the quantitative school. Develops advanced mathematical and statistical tools and techniques for managers.
Matrix management, matrix structure	A hybrid structure that essentially is a project organization superimposed over a functional organization with multiple reporting structures.
Meeting management	Improving the meeting process.
Meeting minutes	Brief, accurate notes of what was discussed in a meeting and the decisions made.
Meeting process	Creating and distributing advance agendas; delineating roles such as leader, facilitator, and scribe; recording and sharing useful meeting minutes; evaluating the meeting process with an eye toward improvement; and completing agreed-upon tasks between meetings.

Mentor	A trusted counselor or teacher.
Milestone	A significant event in the project, usually completion of a major deliverable.
Milestone plan	A summary level plan that identifies major milestones.
Mission statement	A written summary describing why an organization exists.
Monitor	To watch closely the progress of the project; to capture, analyze, and report project performance.
Morale	The state of the spirits of a person or group as exhibited by confidence, cheerfulness, discipline, and willingness to perform assigned project tasks.
Motivate	To provide with an incentive.
Multi-voting	Method whereby each participant votes for whichever approach he or she prefers. The group then progressively removes first the impractical approaches and then the practical but not quite ideal approaches.
Network design document	A network is a series of points or nodes interconnected by communication paths. A network design document shows in detail all the connectivity between the systems and the mode of communication.
Networking	The act of spending time with individuals both inside and outside the project in an effort to develop relationships that may help the project or one's career.
Networking team	Team responsible for networks, system security, and user management.
Objectives	Reason for undertaking the project.
Operating methods	The process of defining working together as a team to prevent some problems from occurring, smooth out difficulties, help the team use time efficiently, make decisions in an atmosphere that minimizes inappropriate conflict, etc. Include decision-making and meeting management.
Orchestrate	To arrange or control the elements. A project leader orchestrates the plan development process so that team members can make discoveries.
Organization	A social entity that is goal-directed and deliberately structured.
Organizational constraint	Restrictions to a project because of organizational policies.
Organizational culture	The culture of the project organization.
Organize	To arrange systematically.
Organizing	The management function that determines how the firm's human, financial, physical, informational, and technical resources are arranged and coordinated to perform tasks to achieve desired goals; the deployment of resources to achieve strategic goals.
Oversee	To watch over and direct.
Paradigm	A mind-set that presents a fundamental way of thinking about perceiving and understanding the world.
Participative leadership, participative decision-making	Leadership that emphasizes consultation with group members and takes their suggestions seriously when making decisions.
Performance	Accomplishment of project expectations; ability to attain goals by using resources efficiently and effectively.

Plan	A formal, approved document used to guide both project execution and project control.
Plan-do-check-act model (PDCA)	The team first plans ("plan")who needs to know what information, how often they need it, and their preferred information format. Next the team uses ("do") the communications plan. Very quickly and repeatedly, the team should seek feedback("check") on the quality and completeness of the information being transmitted through the communications plan. Finally the team should act ("act") on the feedback by improving the communications plan.
Planning	The management function that assesses the management environment to set future objectives and map out activities necessary to achieve those objectives.
Planning stage, project planning	The development and maintenance of the project plan.
Plus delta	A tool for collecting lessons learned. The facilitator draws a large T on a flip chart with a plus sign over the left crossbar and a large triangle over the right crossbar. Then project participants state what they thought was positive and should be repeated during this project or on future projects as well as negative things they feel should be changed.
Political forces	The influence of political and legal institutions on people and organizations.
Polling	Voting, in the form of informal polling; sometimes useful when testing for consensus.
Predecessor	The task prior to the current task in the network diagram.
Preplanning	Preparing the charter; provides a quick understanding of what is involved in completing the potential project with the knowledge that if something is not acceptable, the project may not get approved.
Prioritize	To put things in order of importance.
Problem-solving	The thought processes involved in solving a problem.
Process improvement	Continuous improvement of work processes to achieve project goals and stakeholder satisfaction efficiently and effectively.
Project	A temporary endeavor undertaken to create a unique product, service, or result.
Project charter	A document issued by senior management that formally authorizes the existence of a project. Provides the project manager with the authority to apply organizational resources to project activities.
Project closing	Formalized acceptance of the project and bringing it to an end.
Project kickoff meeting	A formal meeting with the intent of answering all questions and securing approval from all stakeholders to proceed.
Project leader	An individual at any level who exerts a guiding role at some point in a project.
Project lifecycle	A collection of generally sequential project phases whose names and numbers are determined by the control needs of the organization.
Project manager	The individual responsible for managing a project.
Project office	An organizational unit that controls and standardizes project management practices. Some also perform internal training and consulting.
Project sponsor, project champion	A person assigned by top management to mentor the project manager and champion the project, help the project manager secure resources, and help remove obstacles to project progress.
Quality	The totality of characteristics of an entity that bear on its ability to satisfy stated or implied needs.

Quality assurance team, QA team	The team that checks on the project's quality standards.
Recognize	To show awareness of services or appreciate services.
Resources	People, equipment, and materials needed to perform project activities.
Reward	Something given in recognition of exemplary behavior.
Risk	An uncertain event or condition that, if it occurs, has a positive or negative effect on a project's objectives.
Risk assessment	Describes risks under the initial project plan and may indicate areas of needed risk management.
Risk plan	An action plan for managing risks.
Roles	A set of expectations for behavior; describes the extent to which each individual performs activities related to project.
Schedule	The planned dates for performing activities and the planned dates for meeting milestones.
Scientific management	A subfield of the classical management perspective that emphasizes scientifically determined changes in management practices as the solution to improving labor productivity.
Scope	The sum of the products and services to be provided as a project.
Scoring model, weighted scoring model, prioritization matrix	Used when multiple criteria—some more important than others—need to be considered. For example, most people before buying a car will consider several factors such as cost, gas mileage, and style and will weigh them differently.
Scribe	A group member who volunteers to write/record comments on a flip chart.
Situational leadership	Balancing of the needs and concerns of three variables—the leader, the follower, and the situation—in all situations.
Social forces	Aspect of culture that guides and influences relationships among people—their values, needs, and standards of behavior.
SRAM	Static Random Access Memory.
Stakeholders	Individuals and organizations that are actively involved in the project, or whose interests may be positively or negatively affected as a result of project execution or project completion. They may also exert influence over the project and its results.
Steering team	A team of people of vision who see the project in perspective, care about the project's success, and will provide overall guidance and support for the project. In some instances the organization's management team serves this function.
Strategic customer integration initiative	Partnering with a strategically important customer to integrate the supply chain.
Stress test	A test for the computer system to simulate real environment with real volume of data before moving it to production.
Subteam	A smaller team of the core team to work on a project.

Subject matter expert (SME) or extended team member	The individuals who are brought on to the project as needed based on their subject matter expertise.
Supervise	To provide direction.
Supplier-input-process-output-customer model, SIPOC	A tool that can be used to improve the project process by clearly identifying relationships among suppliers, inputs, processes, outputs, and customers.
Supply chain	Fulfillment process from customer purchase through manufacturing, factory, raw material, and component supplier.
Support	To aid the cause.
System	A combination of components working together. For example, a computer system includes both hardware and software.
System requirements document	The document detailing the system specifications for the project.
Systems theory	An approach to understanding how the different elements of an organization function and operate.
Team-building	Developing a common understanding among the team members and developing group competencies to enhance project performance.
Team charter	The document that describes the team operating methods.
Technical architecture design document	The document that shows in detail the architecture of the technical solution.
Technical design specification document	The document that explains the technical design, its business purpose, inputs, outputs, and the technical process.
Technical lead	The person responsible for leading the technical team who is skilled in technology as well as in management.
Technical skill	The understanding of and proficiency in the performance of specific tasks.
Technical team	The team responsible for implementing the technical work of the project.
Terminate project	To make a decision to end work on a project. This can be to end it as planned or to end it prematurely.
Test plans	Test case scenarios written to test the different functionalities of the system and make sure it meets requirements.
Theory Z	A management perspective that incorporates techniques from both Japanese and North American management practices.
Total Quality Management (TQM)	A concept that focuses on managing the total organization to deliver quality to customers. Four significant elements of TQM are employee involvement, focus on the customer, benchmarking, and continuous improvement.
Touchpoints	Places in a project in which work is passed from one person or group to another or when the work of one project intersects the work of another project or the ongoing work of the parent of the customer's organization.

Tradeoff	Deciding which objectives can be sacrificed, enhanced, or maintained, in relation to one another, for the benefit of the overall project.
Trait theory	The theory that suggests that the traits of successful leaders should be studied and emulated.
Transition document	The document that details roles and responsibilities in the day-to-day maintenance of the system.
Use case document	The document describing the use cases that were considered for the system requirements and the use cases that will be tested for customer acceptance of the project.
Virtual fab	The foundry that is connected virtually with all its customers and suppliers to streamline supply chain management.
Vision	Intelligent foresight.
Vote	The act of various project participants expressing their opinion with the aim of being included in the decision-making process.
Wafer	A thin, round slice of a semiconductor material, usually silicon.
Work breakdown structure (WBS)	A deliverable-oriented grouping of project elements that organizes and defines the total work scope of the project. Each descending level represents an increasingly detailed definition of the project work.

Bibliography

Aranda, Eileen K., and Luis Aranda, with Kristi Conlon. *Teams: Structure, Process, Culture, and Politics* (Upper Saddle River, NJ: Prentice Hall, 1998).

Axelrod, Alan. *Patton on Leadership: Strategic Lessons for Corporate Warfare* (Paramus, NJ: Prentice Hall, 1999).

Bechtold, Richard D. *Essentials of Software Project Management* (Vienna, VA: Management Concepts, 1999).

Belasen, Alan T. *Leading the Learning Organization* (Albany, NY: State University of New York Press, 2000).

Bennis, Warren. *On Becoming a Leader* (Reading, MA: Addison-Wesley Publishing Company, 1989).

Bennis, Warren, and Robert Townsend. *Reinventing Leadership: Strategies to Empower the Organization* (New York, NY: William Morrow and Company, Inc., 1995).

Bennis, Warren, Jagdish Parikh, and Ronnie Lessem. *Beyond Leadership: Balancing Economics, Ethics, and Ecology* (Cambridge, MA: Blackwell Business, 1994).

Benton, D.A. *Secrets of a CEO Coach: Your Personal Training Guide to Thinking Like a Leader and Acting Like a CEO* (New York, NY: McGraw-Hill, 1999).

Bergmann, Horst, Kathleen Hurson, and Darlene Russ-Eft. *Everyone a Leader: A Grassroots Model for the New Workplace* (New York, NY: John Wiley & Sons, 1999).

Blanchard, Ken. *Whale Done! The Power of Positive Relationships* (New York, NY: Free Press, 2002).

Blanchard, Ken, and Sheldon Bowles. *Gung Ho: Turn On the People in Any Organization* (New York, NY: Willliam Morrow and Company, Inc., 1998).

Blanchard, Ken, and Sheldon Bowles. *Raving Fans: A Revolutionary Approach to Customer Service* (New York, NY: Free Press, 1993).

Blaylock, Jim, and Rudd McGary. *Project Management Best Practices A to Z* (Colombus, OH: BookMasters, Inc., 2002).

Block, Peter. *Stewardship: Choosing Service over Self-Interest* (San Francisco, CA: Berrett-Koehler Publishers, 1993).

Bouee, Courtland. *Management* (New York: McGraw Hill, 1993).

Burke, Rory. *Project Management: Planning and Control* (NewYork, NY: John Wiley & Sons, 1993).

Bryman, Alan. *Charisma and Leadership in Organizations* (London: Sage Publications, 1992).

Burns, James MacGregor. *Leadership* (Grand Rapids, MI: Harper & Row, 1978).

Chapman, Elwood N. *Leadership: What Every Manager Needs to Know* (New York, NY: Macmillan Publishing Company, 1989).

Clawson, James G. *Level Three Leadership: Getting Below the Surface*, 2nd ed. (Upper Saddle River, NJ: Prentice Hall, 2003).

Cleland, David I. *Field Guide to Project Management* (New York: Van Nostrand Reinhold, 1998).

Cleland, David I. *Project Management: Strategic Design and Implementation*, 2nd ed. (New York: McGraw-Hill, 1994).

Cleland David I., and Lewis R. Ireland. *Project Manager's Portable Handbook* (New York: McGraw-Hill, 2000).

Cleland, David I., James M. Gallagher, and Ronald S. Whitehead. *Military Project Management Handbook* (New York: McGraw-Hill, 1993).

Collins, James C. *Good to Great: Why Some Companies Make the Leap . . . and Others Don't* (New York, NY: HarperCollins, 2001).

Collins, James C., and Jerry I. Porras. *Built to Last: Successful Habits of Visionary Companies* (New York, NY: Harper Business, 1997).

Conger, Jay Alden. *Charismatic Leadership in Organizations* (Thousand Oaks, CA: Sage Publications, 1998).

Covey, Stephen. *The 7 Habits of Highly Effective People* (New York: Simon & Schuster, 1990).

Covey, Stephen R., A. Roger Merrill, and Rebecca R. Merrill. *First Things First* (New York, NY: Simon & Schuster, 1994).

Crawford, J. Kent. *Project Management Maturity Model: Providing a Proven Path to Project Management Excellence* (New York, NY: Marcel Dekker, Inc., 2002).

Crosby, Philip. *The Absolutes of Leadership* (San Diego, CA: Pfeiffer & Company, 1996).

Daft, Richard L. *Management*, 5th ed. (Fort Worth, TX: The Dryden Press, 2000).

Darnall, Russell W. *Achieving TQM on Projects: The Journey of Continuous Improvement* (Upper Darby, PA: Project Management Institute, 1994).

DePree, Max. *Leadership Is an Art* (New York, NY: Dell Publishing, 1989).

Dinkmeyer, Don, and Daniel Eckstein. *Leadership by Encouragement* (Delray Beach, FL: St. Lucie Press, 1996).

Douglass, Merrill E., and Donna N. Douglass. *Time Management for Teams* (New York, NY: American Management Association, 1992).

Esty, Katharine, Richard Griffin, and Marcie Shorr Hirsch. *A Manager's Guide to Solving Problems and Turning Diversity into a Competitive Advantage* (Holbrook, MA: Adams Publishing, 1995).

Fairhurst, Gail T., and Robert A. Sarr. *The Art of Framing: Managing the Language of Leadership* (San Francisco, CA: Jossey-Bass Publishers, 1996).

Gardner, John W. *Excellence: Can We Be Equal and Excellent Too?* (New York, NY: Harper & Row, 1961).

Gardner, John W. *On Leadership* (New York, NY: Free Press, 1990).

Gido, Jack, and James P. Clements. *Successful Project Management* (Cincinnati, OH: South-Western College Publishing, 1999).

Goldman, Daniel. *The Handbook of Emotional Intelligence: Theory, Development, Assessment, and Application at Home, School, and in the Work Place* (San Francisco, CA: Jossey-Bass, 2000).

Goodpasture, John C. *Managing Projects for Value* (Vienna, VA: Management Concepts, 2002).

Gordon, Myron. *How to Plan and Conduct a Successful Meeting* (New York, NY: Sterling Publishing Co., Inc., 1985).

Graham, Robert J., and Randall L. Englund. *Creating an Environment for Successful Projects: The Quest to Manage Project Management* (San Francisco, CA: Jossey-Bass Publishers, 1997).

Gray, Clfford F., and Erik W.Larson. *Project Management: The Managerial Process* (Boston, MA: Irwin McGraw-Hill, 2000).

Greenleaf, Robert K. *The Power of Servant Leadership* (San Fransisco, CA: Berrett-Koehler Publishers, Inc., 1998).

Haas, Howard G., with Bob Tamarkin. *The Leader Within: an Empowering Path of Self-Discovery* (New York, NY: Harper Collins Publishers, 1992).

Harrington, H. James, Daryl R. Conner, and Nicholas L. Horney. *Project Change Management: Applying Change Management to Improvement Projects* (New York, NY: McGraw-Hill, 2000).

Heifetz, Ronald A. *Leadership without Easy Answers* (Cambridge, MA: The Belknap Press, 1994).

Hersey, Paul, and Kenneth Blanchard. *Management of Organizational Behavior*, 4th ed. (Englewood Cliffs, NJ: Prentice Hall, Inc, 1982).

Hesselbein, Frances, Marshall Goldsmith, and Richard Beckhard. *The Leader of the Future* (San Francisco, CA: Jossey-Bass Publishers, 1996).

Holman, Larry. *Eleven Lessons in Self-Leadership: Insights for Personal and Professional Success* (Lexington, KY: A Lessons in Leadership Book, 1995).

Howell, Jon P., and Dan L. Costley. *Understanding Behaviors for Effective Leadership* (Upper Saddle River, NJ: Prentice Hall, 2001).

Hughes, Richard L., Robert C. Ginnett, and Gordon J.Curphy. *Leadership: Enhancing the Lessons of Experience* (Boston, MA: Irwin McGraw-Hill, 1999).

Jacobson, Ivar, Grady Booch, and James Rumbaugh. *The Unified Software Development Process* (Reading, MA: Addison Wesley, 1999).

Katzenbach, Jon R., and Douglas K. Smith. *The Wisdom of Teams: Creating the High-Performance Organization* (New York, NY: Harper Collins Publishers, 1993).

Kerzner, Harold. *In Search of Excellence in Project Management* (Glastonbury, CT: International Thomson Publishing Company, 1998).

Kerzner, Harold. *Project Management: A Systems Approach to Planning, Scheduling, and Controlling,* 7th ed. (New York: John Wiley & Sons, 2001).

Kheng-Hor, Khoo. *Suntzu and Management* (Selangor Darul Ehsan, Malaysia: Pelanduck Publications, 1992).

Kloppenborg, Timothy J. "Project Management," *Encyclopedia of Business* 2nd ed. (Detroit, MI: Gale Research, 1999), 803-806.

Kloppenborg, Timothy J., and Samuel J. Mantel, Jr. "Project Management," *The Concise International Encyclopedia of Business and Management,* 2nd ed. (London: Thompson Press, 2001), 5435–5444.

Kloppenborg, Timothy J., and Samuel J. Mantel. "Tradeoffs on Projects: They Are Not What You Think," *Project Management Journal* 32, no. 1 (1990), 38-53.

Kloppenborg, Timothy J., and Joseph A. Petrick, "Leadership in the Project Life Cycle and Team Character Development, *Project Management Journal* 30, no. 2 (1999), 8-13.

Kloppenborg, Timothy J., and Joseph A. Petrick. *Managing Project Quality* (Vienna, VA: Management Concepts, 2002).

Kloppenborg, Timothy J., and Joseph A. Petrick. "Meeting Management and Group Character Development," *Journal of Managerial Issues* 11, no. 2 (1999), 166-179.

Kloppenborg, Timothy J., Warren A. Opfer, Peter Bycio, Julie Cagle, Thomas Clark, Margaret Cunningham, Miriam Finch, James M. Gallagher, Joseph Petrick, Rachana Sampat, Manar Shami, John Surdick, Raghu Tadepalli, and Deborah Tesch. "Forty Years of Project Management Research: Trends, Interpretations, and Predictions," *Proceedings of PMI Research Conference 2000: Project Management Research at the Turn of the Millennium* (Paris: Project Management Institute, June 21-24, 2000), 41-59.

Knarbanda, O.P., and Jeffrey K. Pinto. *What Made Gertie Gallop: Learning from Project Failure?* (New York, NY: Van Nostrand Reinhold, 1996).

Kostner Jaclyn. *Virtual Leadership: Secrets from the Round Table for the Multi-Site Manager* (New York, NY: Time Warner Books, 1994).

Kuczmarski, Susan Smith, and Thomas D. Kuczmarski. *Values-Based Leadership: Rebuilding Employee Commitment, Performance, and Productivity* (Englewood Cliffs, NJ: Prentice Hall, 1995).

LaFasto, Frank, and Carl E. L*arson. *When Teams Work Best: 6,000 Team Members and Leaders Tell What It Takes to Succeed* (London: Sage Publications, 2001).

Lee, Thomas H., Shoji Shiba, and Chapman Wood. *Integrated Management Systems: A Practical Approach to Transforming Organizations* (New York: John Wiley & Sons, 1999).

Lewis, James P. *Team-Based Project Management* (New York: American Management Association, 1998).

Lindsay, William M., and Joseph A Petrick. *Total Quality and Organization Development* (Delray Beach, FL: St. Lucie Press, 1997).

Locke, Edwin A., and Associates. *The Essence of Leadership: The Four Keys to Leading Successfully* (New York, NY: Lexington Books, 1991).

Lumsden, Gay, and Donald Lumsden. *Communicating in Groups and Teams: Sharing Leadership* (Albany, NY: Wadsworth Publishing Company, 1997).

Mantel, Samuel J., Jr., Jack R. Meredith, Scott M. Shafer, and Margaret M. Sutton. *Project Management in Practice* (New York, NY: John Wiley & Sons, 2001).

Manz, Charles C., and Henry P. Sims. *Super-Leadership: Leading Others to Lead Themselves* (New York, NY: Berkley Books, 1989).

Maxwell, John C. *The 21 Irrefutable Laws of Leadership* (Nashville, TN: Thomas Nelson Publishers, 1998).

Maxwell, John C. *The 21 Most Powerful Minutes in a Leader's Day: Revitalize Your Spirit and Empower Your Leadership* (Nashville, TN: Thomas Nelson Publishers, 2000).

Meadows, Dennis. "The TQM Vital Signs of a Project," *Proceedings of the Project Management Institute* (1998), 18-20.

Meredith, Jack R., and Samuel J. Mantel, Jr. *Project Management: A Managerial Approach*, 4th ed. (New York: John Wiley & Sons, 2000).

Miller, Dennis. *Visual Project Planning and Scheduling* (Boca Raton, FL: The 15th Street Press, Inc., 1994).

Mohrman, Susan, and Allan M. Mohrman, Jr. *Designing and Leading Team-Based Organizations: A Workbook for Organizational Self-Design* (San Francisco, CA: Jossey-Bass Publishers, 1997).

Murch, Richard. *Project Management Best Practices for IT Professionals* (Upper Saddle River, NJ: Prentice Hall, 2001).

Murphy, Emmett C. *Leadership IQ: A Personal Development Process Based on a Scientific Study of a New Generation of Leaders* (New York, NY: John Wiley & Sons, 1996).

Nahavandi, Afsaneh. *The Art and Science of Leadership*, 2nd ed. (Upper Saddle River, NJ: Prentice Hall, 2000).

Napolitano, Carole S., and Lida J. Henderson. *The Leadership Odyssey: A Guide to Self-Development: Guide to New Skills for New Times* (San Francisco, CA: Jossey-Bass Publishers, 1998).

Northouse, Peter G. *Leadership Theory and Practice* (London: Sage Publications, 1997).

Neuendorf, Steve. *Project Measurement* (Vienna, VA: Management Concepts, 2002).

Olson, David L. *Introduction to Information Systems Project Management* (Boston, MA: Irwin McGraw-Hill, 2001).

Orsburn, Jack D., and Linda Moran. *The New Self-Directed Work Teams: Mastering the Challenge* (New York, NY: McGraw-Hill, 2000).

Petrick, Joseph A., and Diana S. Furr. *Total Quality in Managing Human Resources* (Delray Beach: St. Lucie Press, 1995).

Petrick, Joseph A., and John F. Quinn. *Management Ethics: Integrity at Work* (Thousand Oaks, CA: Sage Publications, 1997).

Pinto, Jeffrey K. *Power and Politics in Project Management* (Upper Darby, PA: Project Management Institute, 1996).

Pinto, Jeffrey K. *Project Management Handbook* (San Francisco, CA: Jossey-Bass Publishers, 1998).

Pinto, Jeffrey, and O.P. Kharbanda. *Successful Project Managers: Leading Your Team to Success* (New York, NY: Van Nostrand Reinhold, 1995).

Pinto, Jeffrey K., and Jeffrey W. Trailer. *Leadership Skills for Project Managers* (Newtown Square, PA: Project Management Institute, 1998).

Project Management Institute Standards Committee. *A Guide to the Project Management Body of Knowledge* (Upper Darby, PA: Project Management Institute, 2000).

Reynolds, Joe. *Out Front Leadership: Discovering, Developing, and Delivering Your Potential* (Austin, TX: Bard Productions, 1994).

Ricchiuto, Jack. *Accidental Conversations* (Cleveland, OH: DesigningLife Books, 2002).

Royer, Paul S. *Project Risk Management: A Proactive Approach* (Vienna, VA: Management Concepts, 2002).

Senge, Peter M., Art Kleiner, Charlotte Roberts, Richard B. Ross, and Bryan J. Smith. *The Fifth Discipline Fieldbook: Strategies and Tools for Building a Learning Organization* (New York, NY: Currency Doubleday, 1994).

Scholtes, Peter R., Brian L. Joiner, and Barbara J. Streibel. *The Team Handbook*, 2nd ed. (Madison, WI: Joiner Associates, 1996).

Schuyler, John R. *Decision Analysis in Projects: Learn to Make Faster, More Confident Decisions* (Upper Darby, PA: Project Management Institute, 1996).

Shiba, Shoji, Alan Graham, and David Walden. *A New American TQM: Four Practical Revolutions in Management* (Portland, OR: Productivity Press, 1993).

Shriberg, Arthur, David Shriberg, and Carol Lloyd. *Practicing Leadership: Principles and Applications*, 2nd ed. (New York, NY: John Wiley & Sons, 2001).

Simons, George F., Carmen Vázquez, and Philip R. Harris. *Transcultural Leadership: Empowering the Diverse Workforce* (Houston, TX: Gulf Publishing Company, 1993).

Smith, Hyrum. *The 10 Natural Laws of Successful Time and Life Management: Proven Strategies for Increased Productivity and Inner Peace* (New York, NY: Warner Books, 1994).

Stevens, James D., Timothy J. Kloppenborg, and Charles R Glagola. *Quality Performance Measurements of EPC Process: The Blueprint* (Frankfort, KY: University of Kentucky, 1994).

Tropman, John E. *Making Meetings Work: Achieving High Quality Group Decisions* (Thousand Oaks, CA: Sage Publications, 1996).

Useem, Michael. *The Leadership Moment: Nine True Stories of Triumph and Disaster and Their Lessons for Us All* (New York, NY: Random House, 1998).

Verma, Vijay K. *Human Resource Skills for the Project Manager: The Human Aspects of Project Management* (Upper Darby, PA: Project Management Institute, 1996).

Verma, Vijay K. *Organizing Projects for Success: The Human Aspects of Project Management* (Upper Darby, PA: Project Management Institute, 1995).

Vroom, Victor H., and Arthur G. Jago. *The New Leadership: Managing Participation in Organizations* (Englewood Cliffs, NJ: Prentice Hall, 1998).

Walton, Donald. *Are You Communicating? You Can't Manage Without It* (New York, NY: McGraw-Hill, 1989).

Wilson, Jeanne M., Jill George, and Richard S. Wellins, with William C. Byham. *Leadership Trapeze: Strategies for Leadership in Team-Based Organizations* (San Francisco, CA: Jossey-Bass Publishers, 1994).

Yukl, Gary. *Leadership in Organizations* (Upper Saddle River, NJ: Prentice Hall, 2002).

Index